GLYN EDWARDS

## Books by Glyn Edwards and Santoshan

*The Spirit World in Plain English: Mediumistic and Spiritual Unfoldment* (revised and updated edition of *Tune in to Your Spiritual Potential*)

*Spirit Gems: Essential Guidance for Spiritual, Mediumistic and Creative Unfoldment* (revised and expanded edition of *Unleash Your Spiritual Power and Grow* ~ first published as *21 Steps to Reach Your Spirit*)

### Compiled by Santoshan
*Glyn Edwards: The Potential of Mediumship*
*~ A Collection of Essential Teachings and Exercises (expanded edition)*

*Reflections with Glyn Edwards*
*~ With additional material by Santoshan (expanded edition)*

### Santoshan, with conversations with Glyn Edwards
*Realms of Wondrous Gifts: Psychic, Mediumistic and Miraculous Powers in the Great Mystical and Wisdom Traditions (revised edition)*

\* \* \*

### Other Titles by Santoshan

*Rivers of Green Wisdom:*
*Exploring Christian and Yogic Earth Centred Spirituality*

*Spirituality Unveiled: Awakening to Creative Life*

*From Punk Rock to Green Spirituality (a collection of articles)*

### Coauthored with Swami Dharmananda Saraswati
*The House of Wisdom: Yoga Spirituality of the East and West*
*(with an introduction by Glyn Edwards)*

### Compiled by Santoshan
*GreenSpirit Reflections (multi-authored)*

*Pathways of Green Wisdom: Discovering Earth Centred Teachings in Spiritual and Religious Traditions (multi-authored)*

### Compiled with Ian Mowll
*Awakening to Earth-Centred Consciousness:*
*Selection from GreenSpirit Magazine (multi-authored)*

*Dark Nights of the Green Soul: From Darkness to New Horizons*
*(multi-authored)*

# Glyn Edwards

A renowned medium remembered
*Collection of memories and teachings*

Compiled by Santoshan (Stephen Wollaston)

Published by S Wollaston, 2019
Independent publishing platform

Copyright © 2019 Santoshan (Stephen Wollaston)
ISBN:
979-8479749162 (hardback) / 978-0956921048 (paperback)
1st edition
Amazon hardback 2021 / paperback 2020

A CIP record of this book is available from the British Library

All rights reserved. Except for brief quotations in critical articles or reviews, no part of this book may be reproduced in any manner without prior written permission from the publisher.
The rights of the authors have been asserted in accordance with the Copyright, Designs and Patents Act 1988.

Design and artwork by Santoshan (Stephen Wollaston)

Copyright on all photos, which were taken by Santoshan (Stephen Wollaston), except those on pages 13 by Tony Stewart, 19 by Eileen Davies, 30 by a student and 52 by Mark Stone.

Front cover photo: Glyn in East London. Late summer of 1989.
Back cover photo: Glyn on a weekend break in Nottingham, near Sherwood Forest. Mid-October 2010.

# Contents

Preface 7
Introduction 9
Glyn Edwards (biography) 13

**PART ONE: MEMORIES & TRIBUTES**

1. Personal Stories and Reflections:

Glyn's Help with My Unfoldment ~ Ron Jordan (Devadūta) 21
Meeting Glyn at the Arthur Findlay College ~ Morag MacLellan 22
A Message from Glyn in Australia ~ Joanne Becker 26
A "Short" Appreciation of a Unique Human Being
~ Susan Farrow 31
Remembering Glyn ~ Carole Lynne 33
Some Treasured Memories ~ Janet Glasgow 36
The Purple Silk Dress ~ Geoffrey Saunders 38
Memories of a Beautiful Man ~ Jane Roberts 40
A Deep and Long Friendship ~ Santoshan (Stephen Wollaston) 43
Shared Memories and Grateful Thanks ~ Mark Stone 48
Glyn at Longton Spiritualist Church ~ Kathryn Shirley 53
Spirit Ambassador ~ Micky Havelock 56

**PART TWO: SELECTION OF TEACHINGS & REFLECTIONS BY GLYN EDWARDS**

2. Intuitive Arts 61
3. Varieties of Unfolding Mediumistic Experience 67
4. Meetings with a Yoga Master 77
5. Realms of Knowing 87
6. Exercises 95

**Afterword: Writing with Glyn 109**
**Books and Recordings by or with Glyn Edwards 111**

## WORKSHOP SECTIONS
*Guidance of the Spirit 65*
*Patterns of Mediumistic Experience 73*
*Beliefs and Believing 74*
*Things to Consider for Mediumistic Unfoldment 93*
*Your Interrelationship with Earth Life and the Spirit World 105*
*A Kaleidoscope of Mediumship 106*

**Information for photos of Glyn Edwards on the below pages:**

Page 13: Taken by one of the pillars leading to the Arthur Findlay College Sanctuary in 1999, for the back cover of 'Tune in to Your Spiritual Potential' (revised and retitled in 2011 as 'The Spirit World in Plain English').

Page 20: Taken in the Arthur Findlay College grounds, by the tulip tree, in 2002.

Page 59: Glyn on holiday in Spain, at Granada in 1989.

Page 111: Taken in East London in 2001.

# Preface

After collaborating on four book projects with Glyn, it was only natural for people to ask if I had considered doing a biographical one about him after his passing. I did in fact write a more detailed short biography about Glyn for an expanded edition of *The Potential of Mediumship* anthology of his wisdom, which was released in 2017, and have also included it in the following pages as it felt fitting to do so. As far back as the 90s, when friends got wind of Glyn and me working on our first book they often assumed it was going to be a biography about his life. It was not as if the suggestion had not been put to him, and it would not have been that hard to put together while being in touch with him so regularly. However, much to Glyn's credit, he was never interested in a book along those lines being written about him, and was always about the teachings of the spirit, his public work and helping others. His prime focus was on the spirit world's interrelationship with numerous interwoven spheres of unfoldment, and on practical down-to-earth wisdom and practices.

Yet in addition to enquiries from people about a biography of Glyn's life, different people approached me about the possibility of an anthology of this kind, which shares personal thanks, experiences, stories and memories about Glyn, alongside a collection of chapters of his teachings. I decided to run the idea of possibly taking on the task past a few of Glyn's colleagues and friends, as well as his sister and youngest brother. The response I got was instantly positive; everyone offered encouragement and felt it would be a wonderful tribute to him and his work. One of the people I spoke to was Reverend Andreas Hindström from Sweden, who kindly offered to help in being the first port of call for anyone with a story or memory to share. This made my role in putting this book together a smoother ride, for which I am grateful and wish to thank Andreas for his help, as it allowed me time to focus on the compiling, editing, proofreading and design. He, along with Mark Stone – another of Glyn's friends who I also wish to thank for assisting with proofreading – were also helpful for being people I could run ideas past about things I was considering including.

I have aimed at giving readers an array of bitesized memories about Glyn and things he wrote and taught. The second part of this anthology is where different articles, talk extracts, workshop sections and exercises by Glyn are to be found, including an amazing account of several fascinating meetings he had with a Yoga master and a collection of key quotations from Glyn's published works. In the majority of this material, Glyn frequently shares insightful personal reflections and experiences about his own mediumistic and spiritual unfoldment. The majority of memories and stories in the first part have been written from the heart. I trust readers will find the memories shared by contributors, along with the chapters by Glyn, a source of upliftment and something to treasure. Glyn touched many people's lives in so many ways. The recollections people have shared have been a means for them to give something back and show deep-felt appreciation of Glyn's work and friendship and the impact he had on their lives.

\* \* \*

# Introduction

Glyn was internationally known and respected for having a deep passion for doing mediumistic work and teaching and had great presence on stage, including a strong public voice with a rich tone that grabbed people's attention. Detailed and accurate evidence of human survival after death often seemed to flow effortlessly for him. People attended his courses and workshops just as much for his wisdom, charisma and dynamic presence as a motivational speaker and extraordinary orator as they did for his reputation as an outstanding medium. He sometimes ran development courses and spiritual retreats at the Arthur Findlay College in Essex that did not include mediumship at all, but other paths and practices that focused on Eastern and Western spirituality, and were just as popular as the ones he ran on mediumistic unfoldment.

He remains one of very few people, apart from megastars, royalty, and leaders of countries and world religions, that I have seen sparking a spontaneous and rapturous standing ovation from an audience of around 50 people, just for walking into a packed small hall before saying or doing anything! It occurred at the start of an evening's demonstration of mediumship with Glyn at the Seekers Trust in Kent in 2011. There was a young German student that both Glyn and I knew in the audience, who turned to me with a beaming smile on her face after observing the enthusiastic welcome. We were both touched by the audience's unprompted appreciation of someone we knew so well.

When Glyn was not publicly working, he liked planning holidays and spiritual retreats, and going to places where he could relax in natural settings and be energised by different cultures and ways of being at peace. Included in his mediumistic and spiritual life was a fervent love of Earth-centred spirituality. As well as being a renowned medium, teacher and orator with an inclusive interfaith approach to his work, he can also be looked upon as a Nature mystic because of the experiences he often had when he was deeply aware of the natural world's sentient life and reconnected with Gaia's awesome creativity and beauty. Even when meeting people's pets, he would show great fondness of their presence and personality and was always joyous in his interactions with them. He always made me smile when he greeted and enthusiastically talked to animal friends.

Because of his understanding of the natural world, he never denied the importance of physical life, but affirmed its spiritual essence and saw how the spirit world was profoundly interwoven with the creativity of all. He taught and wrote about various interrelated spheres of mediumistic phenomena and spirituality, which he wove around an array of insights from a coat of many colours. At times, he found it restrictive working within the framework of the Spiritualist movement, as he often felt the need to go beyond labels and boundaries, which is another noticeable theme running through his teachings.

He was refreshingly progressive and always enthusiastically embracing new and *helpful* insights people had had and broadening his understanding and wisdom. Some of the things he taught in the early 90s is different to what he taught 20 years later, which is to be expected when someone is authentically open to ongoing creative development. He was particularly drawn and had experiences connected to Yogic, Buddhist and Christian mystical teachings and practices, and enjoyed engaging in mutually beneficial dialogues with people from diverse fields of spirituality and finding common ground. His open-minded inclusiveness and search for an interspiritual perennial wisdom, in fact, profoundly enriched both his mediumistic and spiritual life and gave them deeper meaning and purpose.

He was generally down-to-earth and practical in his life and work and helped others whenever he could. Yet when it came to publicly demonstrating his mediumistic abilities, he usually broke the rule of staying on the podium and often walked up to people in the congregation to deliver a message from spirit. Sometimes he would turn to people in the audience who had lost direction in their life or were at crossroads, informing them that he had to speak to them and that it was not about evidence of survival after death, as that was not what they needed at that time, but guidance about what was going on at the moment. There were numerous occasions like this when Glyn stepped outside of traditional expectations of mediumistic work, which readers will notice in some of his teachings and this book's tributes to him.

Like a lot of public figures and gay men, he often dressed well and paid attention to his appearance. He spent much of his public life promoting an engaged spirituality relevant for our times and encouraged others to be as wide, accepting and universal in their search for spiritual truths and growth as he had been. He was aware that we live in multicultural societies with neighbours from various faiths and disparate forms of sexual orientation, and need to look upon everyone as a part of our global spiritual community, as our sisters and brothers, which includes the animal queendoms and kingdoms.

Like all of us, he was not perfect and spoke openly about his own personal struggles. A friend commented just after Glyn's passing, how brave he was. Not only for blazing a trail for what he believed in and aimed to live out and embody in his life, but also for how he handled physical adversity. He had had hearing problems since he was a child, which he never allowed to get in the way of achieving what he sought to accomplish. A mystery illness he contracted in 2003 was at first devastating for him. Initially, it took lots of support from close friends, medical staff and his family for him to pick himself up and heal, but once he did, he quickly started to work again and seemed to find richer levels to his mediumship, spirituality and teaching. Even more remarkable was the dignity and valour he displayed in handling the onset of cancer in the last year of his Earth life. Right up to the very last week, his sense of humour and his enthusiasm for working with students and the spirit were as much in evidence as they had ever been. He most certainly walked his talk in so many different and amazing ways. I can only hope that readers will come to appreciate and be inspired by his incredible work and life in the following pages.

~ Santoshan (Stephen Wollaston)

\* \* \*

**Awakening to evolving and eternal life**
Unity in diversity  Limitless potential
**The whole self**  Compassionate growth
**Oneness with the spirit world**
Awareness  Original goodness  Co-creativity
Nature as an expression of divinity and part of us
Living by spiritual laws

*Above: Word cloud of some key areas in Glyn's teachings.*

# Glyn Edwards

*In the course of my development I have come to realise how our individual spirit, Nature, the spirit world and God are continuously creating, and how by participating with this activity we become co-creators with the creative powers of all life.*
~ GLYN EDWARDS

Glyn Edwards was born in Liverpool on 17th August 1949 and was the oldest of four siblings. His parents, Violet and Eddie, came from Catholic and Welsh Presbyterian Church backgrounds. As Glyn's father was in the army, Glyn spent a lot of his early years living in different parts of the world such as Cyprus and Egypt. His parents then settled for a while in the UK when Eddie, with Violet's help, became a pub landlord in Aylesbury, Buckinghamshire. They then lived in the United States for a period, but Glyn remained in England.

---

Note: This biography is from the anthology of Glyn's wisdom *The Potential of Mediumship (expanded edition)*.

During his Earth life, Glyn became internationally recognised as one of the UK's finest mediums. At 16 he joined a Benedictine community. Within this period of his life, various mediumistic experiences he had had since a child intensified, which subsequently led him to leave the community after staying for two years. He then went on to train at Sassoon's, became a sought-after hairdresser and began to take a deeper interest in his mediumistic abilities after a sitting under an assumed name with a medium who gave him remarkable evidence about his grandmother and other members of his family.

After doing his first public demonstration of mediumship at 19, he immediately went on to working regularly as a medium. He later became a certificated medium of the SNU (Spiritualists' National Union) and a protégée of the world renowned medium Gordon M Higginson, and worked on an array of projects with him for many years, including demonstrating his mediumship at the Derby Assembly Rooms in 1991 as part of the SNU's centenary celebrations.

He travelled extensively, speaking, lecturing, demonstrating and running workshops throughout the UK and worldwide for over 40 years. He owed much of his early work to Jean Matheson, a long-time friend and organiser of numerous successful events and courses in the north of England, who sat for him in a highly productive development circle and helped him gain confidence in his abilities.

He was the main founder of the Gordon Higginson Fellowship and the Gordon Higginson Awareness Foundation, both of which ran various courses in the south of England. He was also a regular course organiser and teacher at the Arthur Findlay College for over three decades, worked at the Spiritualist Association of Great Britain, and was involved with the research of PRISM (Psychical Research Involving Selected Mediums).

He possessed extensive understanding of various mediumistic and spiritual paths, and was always up-to-date with the latest ideas and discoveries of different traditions. He was particularly known for the quality of his work and his ability to demonstrate his mediumship almost effortlessly in front of large audiences. A short YouTube video of Glyn publicly demonstrating his mediumship, taken from a documentary shown on the BBC about the SNU, shows him giving evidence that even the most hardened sceptic would find difficult to explain away about a town where someone used to live having "a very unusual post box", as it wasn't painted red, "it was green and made out of wood!"

On some occasions he gave a demonstration of trance mediumship. More than anything, Glyn was highly respected for his understanding of and insight into different areas of mediumistic unfoldment and his devotion to helping students explore and realise their individual potential. His teachings and courses often promoted an inclusive approach to development. Along with those from Spiritualist backgrounds, students and teachers on his courses and workshops could come from a variety of traditions such as Hindu, Christian, Jewish, Yogic, Buddhist, Sufi, Psychotherapist, Reiki Healer and Neo-Pagan, and could be of any age from teenage years to senior citizens.

He was interviewed on television and radio throughout the world, recorded many teachings and practices, wrote numerous articles on mediumship and spiritual growth, and coauthored two development manuals (*Tune in to Your Spiritual Potential* and *21 Steps to Reach Your Spirit*). Because of other commitments Glyn had and the slow process of publishing in the 90s, the first book took eight years from conception to being released in printed form. Nonetheless, Glyn worked on several of his chapters while on a single two week holiday in the New Forest area in south England. The two coauthored books were thoroughly revised and given new titles in 2011: *The Spirit World in Plain English* and *Spirit Gems*. Glyn was also extensively featured in two in-depth interviews in the book *Realms of Wondrous Gifts*,[1] released in 2008, and featured in a book called *The Best of British*, which was released to coincide with the new millennium.

In order to recharge his own batteries, Glyn frequently went on silent retreats to various countryside and town monasteries in the UK. For a while, he undertook instruction from a renowned Tantric Yoga master, Sri Jammu Maharaj, as well as a teacher from the Bihar School of Yoga, Swami Dharmananda Saraswati Maharaj, who gave him the name Devadasa (meaning servant of God). Along with Eastern wisdom and practices such as Mindfulness, Glyn was for many years deeply inspired by the teachings of the New Thought writer and teacher Ernest Holmes, took serious interest in the revival of Centring Prayer pioneered by Thomas Keating, and found times being amongst Nature an important part of his spiritual life. Two of his favourite places to go on holiday were the Lake District in the north of England, and Devon in the south. Insights about the creativity of Nature, an ever-present spirit world and the divinity in all were often predominant themes in Glyn's talks and writings.

He had a deep passion for reading about different spiritual paths; his modest apartment in Maids Moreton, Buckinghamshire, was like a wonderful library of universal

---

1. Glyn especially requested the *Realms* book to be done, and for it to be published by the Gordon Higginson Fellowship, one of the organisations Glyn founded. A new revised and redesigned edition was released in 2018.

wisdom. He also had a great love of art, live theatre, poetry, and various styles of music, particularly the joyousness that is often expressed in JS Bach's compositions, and the sublime vocal skills of the Indian singer Kaushiki Chakrabarty. Both Bach and Chakrabarty were often found to be playing more than any other CDs on Glyn's car stereo.

In 2003 he made the front page of Psychic News (which he had done many times in his mediumistic life) after being struck down by a mystery illness that affected the muscles on the left side of his face as well as his balance and often used a stick for walking from then on. After this, he showed how determination and the power of the spirit can overcome adversity. Remarkably, many testified to how his work and teachings moved on to a deeper level. He personally found this chapter in his life opening up many profound insights and experiences that expanded his mediumistic and spiritual understanding.

In the late spring of 2014 he was diagnosed with cancer and underwent chemotherapy. Although it became clear Glyn was not responding well to the treatment, he insisted on teaching up to the last and even began an outline for an article from his hospital bed towards the end of his Earth life. He remained positive and passed to spirit peacefully with his mother and sister, Elaine, by his side at 10am on 31st May 2015. A service for close friends and family was held in the morning at Crownhill Crematorium, Milton Keynes, on 12th June. A celebration of his life was especially held in the afternoon at Akeley Village Hall for public attendance and to coincide with his youngest brother, Delwyn, and one of Glyn's best friends being in the UK at the same time.

People whose lives had been touched by Glyn came from as far as Scotland, Germany, Sweden and Holland. Ian Mowll, an interfaith minister, led the afternoon celebration, during which family members, respected mediums and close friends of Glyn's such as Eileen Davies and Mark Stone shared treasured memories about him. Other celebration and memorial services and remembrances of Glyn's life were also organised, including one at the Greater Boston Church of Spiritualism in the United States, and one by the SNU at the Arthur Findlay College on its Open Week in 2016, which was written about in Psychic News and accompanied by an article about Glyn, his life, loves and individual spiritual growth.

Glyn's work lives on of course in his books (including a new book of inspiring quotations by him),[2] recordings and with various people and students he helped, many of whom have become teachers and mediums because of Glyn's help. There have even been reports of him communicating via some working mediums and mediumistic development circles, and the Glyn Edwards Spiritual Awareness Foundation ran many popular courses honouring his name for five years after his passing.

*   *   *

---

[2]. Titled *Reflections with Glyn Edwards*, which was released in 2019 to coincide with what would have been Glyn's 70th Earth-year.

PART ONE

# Memories & Tributes

Photo taken by the medium Eileen Davies, who was a close friend of Glyn's, of Kingswells' memory table, which was devoted to Glyn. After Glyn's passing, whenever Kingswells had a course at the centre, he was always remembered and a part of all they did there.

# 1
# Personal Stories and Reflections

## Glyn's Help with My Unfoldment
### by Ron Jordan (Devadūta)

It was many years ago as a young man that I first met Glyn. He liked the way I delivered my mediumship and asked me if I would like to teach on some of his courses. We then spent a couple of hours talking about the way I'd developed my mediumship up to that point. He then asked me to give him a message, which I at first thought was a bit unusual, but afterwards he told me that as well as being clairaudient (the ability to hear spirit personalities) at that time, I also had the potential for being clairvoyant (the ability to see spirit personalities), which Glyn said he would help me bring to the fore and mentioned how it would benefit my overall mediumship.

Over many months, Glyn taught me different techniques that eventually altered my ability to communicate greatly. As well as this, he also taught me various beneficial meditation techniques that he himself had found helpful and been introduced to on his own spiritual and mediumistic journey by teachers from different traditions. I discovered that the techniques helped to change my sensitivity to and quickened my contact with the spirit world.

At that time, nobody knew just how much Glyn had helped me, but people saw the difference when I worked. In contrast to the impression people might have got from his dynamic public image as a working medium, he was not a boastful man and never told anyone what he did for people he liked, respected and called a friend; he just kept giving his knowledge and sharing his experiences with those he knew would pass it on as freely as he had given it.

In all the years I knew and whenever I worked alongside Glyn, he was one of the most caring and kind people I had ever met. His knowledge of the spirit world was outstanding, and his ability to take novice students and give them insights into their own potential was wonderful to witness time and time again.

Many people are not aware how outstanding a medium and teacher Glyn in fact was. As well as his public work, his highly beneficial books and recordings have helped countless people become more aware of their own spiritual potential and introduced them to the many wonders of the spirit. There are no adequate words to express the void that has been left without his physical presence, but knowing Glyn, he will be with the great teachers who passed before him, discussing spiritual matters and passionately sharing his own individual wisdom. As he always did!

\* \* \*

## Meeting Glyn at the Arthur Findlay College
### by Morag MacLellan

I first met Glyn Edwards in that tiny lift at Stansted Hall, the home of the Arthur Findlay College in Essex, South-East England, the world's foremost college for the advancement of Spiritualism and psychic science. That lift, in common with many shoehorned, retrospectively, into historic buildings, is very snug, and feels full if it holds only two or three people. I found myself faced with a strange man, holding up his forearms towards me and asking for help. I quickly realised that his shirt cuff buttons were undone and he needed me to fasten them up for him. It was a touchingly intimate moment, shared with a complete stranger. Although I didn't realise it at the time, we were both on our way to the Sanctuary where services are held at the college, where Glyn was to give a demonstration of mediumship.

I first met with my friends, Chris and Heather. Chris hails from Scotland, like me, and Heather travelled with me from Canada to study at the AFC – we were taking a course that week led by Libby Clark. We three girls sat at the back of the Sanctuary, which was filling up fast, and I remember thinking we looked like three naughty school kids at the back of the class.

The demonstration began, messages coming through beautifully, swiftly and organically. I was surprised to note that Glyn did not stay on the platform. After several visits to the college, I was aware that stepping off the platform during a demonstration was a rule not to be broken. But here Glyn was, advancing up the aisle towards us. Suddenly his attention came to me. He brought through my father, and gave lots of unusual evidence, very personal and intimate things, between the two of us. He shared this information in a manner that did not cause me any embarrassment. I was touched and truly felt the presence of my father. The really stunning part for me, and my two companions, was when Glyn related word for word a conversation we three had had at lunch that day. This, for me, was a clear demonstration that my father saw and heard our recent activities.

Glyn then switched his attention to Chris, who was sitting the other side of Heather, who was piggy in the middle, and brought through her father. He gave Chris lots of great information that she could relate to, and she too was stunned by his accuracy. Now and again he switched back to me to add something from my father. Heather sitting in the middle looked like she was watching a tennis match at Wimbledon. Glyn was amazingly linking to both of our Scottish fathers simultaneously, deftly switching back and forth with the correct evidence landing with the right daughter. We were all stunned and Heather and I determined there and then to come on one of Glyn's courses or one of which he was listed as a main co-tutor the following year as I was so struck by the accuracy and natural, seemingly effortless delivery of his mediumship that I knew I needed and wanted to learn from him. There was one listed at a good time of year for us, called Mediumship, Prophecy and Mysticism, I believe, which we booked immediately.

Sadly, it was not to be. Glyn passed to spirit a couple of weeks before the course began. Eileen Davies was the course leader, and there was a palpable sense of loss amongst the tutors and students who knew him, some for three decades. I realised that the man I met in the tiny lift had had a huge influence on Spiritualism and been an important part of the spiritual and mediumistic development of so many.

Heather and I went to the college bookshop and bought all the available works by Glyn they stocked. During that first week, Libby Clark, the tutor of the group I was in, asked me to facilitate an evening workshop for the Friends of Stansted Hall, which meets on a Wednesday in the Pioneer Centre in the grounds of the college. Heather and I were welcomed by our friend Rachel Casson, and introduced to the group members. Heather and I sat next to each other and decided to dedicate our workshop to the memory of Glyn, which seemed fitting and so we chose the Sitting in the Power meditation from one of our newly acquired books, *Glyn Edwards: The Potential of Mediumship*, compiled and with an introduction by Santoshan.

We had just finished the meditation and were quietly waiting for the participants to slowly return their attention to the room, when we spotted an enormous fly coming straight towards Heather and I while we were still sitting close to each other. It flew straight between our two heads. We were both aware of stories about Glyn's mischievous humour and immediately turned to each other and said, "Glyn?" Then we started to giggle. And then looking around, we realised that our flying friend had completely disappeared! The door was closed and no window was open. It just vanished! We were both convinced it was a warm-hearted and playful message from Glyn, showing his approval.

We heard that Glyn had also come through that week to a new AFC student, to someone who knew nothing about him, his life or recent passing. That made sense as pure evidence, untainted by memory or reputation. We had the privilege during the week to attend a service in the Sanctuary of the college that was originally planned to have been led by Glyn himself, but was now a remembrance service honouring his life and work. Many of his close friends were there to pay their respects and to tell stories, often hilarious ones, about this incredible man. I loved hearing about one of his sayings: Be Marvellous, Be Bold, Be You! This is great advice for any medium, as we are tasked with conquering ourselves.

I have since used the books Glyn did with his friend Santoshan a lot in my own mediumistic development and in my teaching, and have sometimes felt Glyn's presence, particularly in difficult times, encouraging me to be brave and embrace life's difficulties with wisdom, as he himself did when faced with challenges and remarkably remained positive and publicly active right up to the very end of his amazing Earth life. This seems to me to be the very embodiment of Be Bold, Be Marvellous, Be You!

Sometimes our lives touch but briefly, and the influence is profound and there to stay. Thank you, Glyn, for all that you are, and shall ever be.

\* \* \*

## A Message from Glyn in Australia
### *by Joanne Becker*

I had just been to the Victoria Spiritualists Union's Sunday Service and had been underwhelmed by the evidence offered by the mediums that day. A lady I hardly knew called Kerry asked me if I wanted to see Glyn Edwards – a British medium who was visiting Melbourne. Could I be bothered coming back into town on what might be another disappointing event? Hmmm… Oh well, I had tried the amateurs, I might as well try the professionals. "Okay", I said. "What time and where will I meet you?"

Anyway, in typical Joanne fashion, I cut it fine and was a wee bit late. We went upstairs and there were only two seats left. They were in the very, very last row at the back of the jam-packed hall. Kerry and I sat down. The place was buzzing. Glyn's messages were chalk and cheese in comparison to other mediums who had been at the church service. They were so specific. I sat there incredulous. This couldn't be right surely? How did he know all this stuff?

I vividly recall one of his messages. He came to a woman a few rows from me. "May I come to you madam?" Glyn asked in a booming voice. "Yes", said the woman. "I have your husband here. You used to call him Bang Bang because he used to thump on the piano keyboard. You are worried because your daughter wishes to change schools", etc, etc.

I thought "Oh My God. This is so specific. These people have to be plants. This can't be real". Then the person running the night said "One last reading Glyn": I put all my power into the thought "Pick me, pick me, pick me" and tried to push the thought to him as strongly as I could "PICK ME".

Glyn said, "Can I come to the woman in the black at the back?" I looked around. "You madam."

Eeeekkkkk. "Yes."

Now because I was at the back, every single person in the room turned around to look at me. I might as well have been on stage.

The beginning of my reading was different from every other reading he had done that night. Glyn said, "Oh my lips are so sore. You can have that back".

How did he know that? My lips were killing me. Hmmm, maybe they were swollen or something.

Glyn said, "Oh and my back is sore right here" and pointed to a spot. He asked "Do you understand that?"

"Hmmm…maybe."

Glyn appeared cross/frustrated. "It's either yes or no."

I replied, "Well, it was a few days ago".

The whole room erupted into laughter. Evidently a few days doesn't matter when it comes to a reading. I had been moving furniture and had hurt my back in a very weird specific place.

How had he known that? Hmmm, maybe I was sitting funny or something.

There was one other physical concern I had that day…
He said, "Oh and there's something else but I don't think we'll share that".

"NO." I said panicked (I had constipation lol).

Then he said, "Three months ago you broke up with someone you had been going out with for six years".

Oh my God. How the heck did he know that? No one in that room knew that. The woman Kerry probably didn't even know my last name. She did not know my telephone number or address. She wasn't a close friend at the time and didn't know that, and I knew no others in this room. I had told no one and I mean no one that I was coming along that night. The words Spiritualist Church had never crossed my lips. I wasn't a plant. There was no Facebook or Internet back then. No email. How did he know that?

Then he said a personal message. "There are two women always with you. They are relatives on your mother's side. They died within days of each other, around about Easter. Do you know who I mean?"

"Nope." I replied. I had absolutely no idea.

Glyn stopped and looked like he was listening to someone and then he said, "No, you don't but your parents do. Ask your parents".

Then he stopped and sniffed the air. He said, "There is a great smell of lavender".

Wow. So how do I find out about these women? I rang my mum.

"Hi Mum. I want to do the family tree…" We went through births and dates of a few people and just when we got to the interesting part Mum said "No! You have been to the Spiritualist Church. I am not going to tell you" and hung up.

Now, how the heck did Mum know? I still hadn't told anybody. I still hadn't said the words Spiritualist Church to anyone. Kerry was the only one who knew this and she didn't know my mum's phone number, where mum lived. She didn't even know where I lived.

Time went by.

It was about five years later or so and I was visiting mum in New Zealand. I was doing the dishes in the kitchen with my Aunty Gaye (mum's sister) when the reading suddenly occurred to me.

"Aunty Gaye, do you know two female relatives who died within days of each other around about Easter?"

"Yes. Your great grandmother and Aunty Sarah."

"Anything stand out about either of them?"

"Yes. Aunty Sarah loved lavender."

\* \* \*

*Glyn giving a demonstration of mediumship at the Derby Assembly Rooms in 1991 as part of the Spiritualists' National Union's centenary celebrations.*

Glyn on holiday in the Lake District, England, with close friends Jean Matheson and the renowned medium and former president of the Spiritualists' National Union, Gordon Higginson. Early October 1990.

Glyn chairing a day that he helped to promote on Co-creative Spirituality with Cosmologist Chris Clarke, Interfaith Minister and GreenSpirit Coordinator Ian Mowll, and Santoshan at the Seekers Trust, Kent. Early spring 2010.

## A "Short" Appreciation of a Unique Human Being
### *by Susan Farrow*

To write an appreciation of the unique human being that was Glyn Edwards would require a book. How to sum up such a complex mixture of talent, passion, spirituality, courage, determination and sheer kindness in a few brief paragraphs?

I probably knew Glyn for fewer years than many who have written about him. I encountered him as a medium, as an interview subject on several occasions, and subsequently as a most generous friend. He was enormously supportive of my work as editor of Psychic News – we shared a passion for high evidential standards and integrity in mediumship, along with a mission to root out those who brought it into disrepute.

There is little I can say in praise of his public demonstrations of mediumship that will not already have been said by many others. Few would disagree that his was a towering talent. What I can do, though, is to share an enduring memory of what proved to be a private sitting of extraordinary value to me.

I chose Glyn because of his huge natural ability, and also because, at that stage, he didn't know me very well. I was in a situation most of us face at some time or another: I knew that a major life change was necessary, I even knew what it was but had no idea how to facilitate it, was deeply confused, sleep-deprived and worried sick. Glyn knew nothing of this before the sitting.

We sat down in Santoshan's flat and Glyn was quiet for a long time. Excellent evidence of my partner followed – he had passed to spirit six years previously. I was delighted, of course, but it did not address the unrelated situation on which I had hoped to receive guidance. Another period of quiet ensued.

Suddenly, Glyn sat bolt upright in his chair and detailed my situation to the letter.

I am an old hand at all this, but I was stunned. There followed a detailed description of where I would live, what I would be doing, complications that were preventing these events from unfolding and causing me such restlessness, and how they would be resolved. Within a little over a year, every one of those predictions had come true. It was a spectacular example of mediumship at its finest.

Glyn's diagnosis of cancer in 2014 was for obvious reasons a bitter blow to him and caused him to think deeply about many spiritual and philosophical issues. It must have been an extraordinarily challenging time for him, and even as he underwent treatment he twice made the long drive from Buckinghamshire to the West Midlands to visit and talk with my companion Minister Eric Hatton, for whom he had enormous respect and affection. The conversations and reflections that unfolded were some of the most honest and profound I can ever remember, and it was a privilege to have a small part in them.

A few weeks after the second of those visits, while Glyn's arduous and debilitating treatment continued, Eric himself was diagnosed with cancer. His doctors determined that he would need radical surgery, but a nine-hour operation at the age of 88 was no small matter. After many weeks of further consultations and risk assessments he was admitted to hospital for the long-awaited surgery. It was a difficult and stressful time.

Throughout it there was one person who phoned me nearly every day to see how Eric was doing. That person was Glyn Edwards, sometimes calling from his own hospital bed. I have never forgotten, and will never forget, that colossal generosity of spirit. It was the single most unselfish display of caring friendship that I have ever encountered.

*   *   *

### Remembering Glyn
*by Carole Lynne* CSNU

If I could have actually seen Glyn's energy field, I'm sure it would have been huge. His voice was resounding, his personality penetrating, and his ideas stirred up my thoughts. What a gift it was for me to have spent time with him on several memorable occasions. So how did this happen?

Nancy Garber, CSNU (Certificate of the Spiritualists' National Union), arranged for many British mediums to visit the Boston area. She asked me if I would host Glyn at my house. I'd seen him do demonstrations of mediumship at the Arthur Findlay College in Essex in England where I was once a student, and also at the Quincy and Watertown Spiritualist Churches in the Boston area. I already knew that Glyn was a powerful medium and had a strong presence, so when I accepted the offer to host him at my house, I was both excited and a bit nervous.

When he arrived, I was enthralled with the opportunity to sit with him outside while he smoked a cigarette, as he did at that time, share breakfast with him and chat in-between his many activities while staying at my place. I found him to be so knowledgeable and dedicated to communicating with spirit. He was passionate about spirit communication as well as spiritual growth as a whole. I also found him to be one of the most sensitive and charismatic people I'd ever met. I wondered how anyone could manage that amount of power deeply flowing through his or her being.

Honestly, and of course this is only my personal opinion, I

think he was truly blessed with the abilities he had, which, I feel, most individuals would find hard to handle and remain level-headed. I did wonder sometimes about how such a powerful person could maintain a balanced life, both physically and emotionally. From my perspective, he seemed to be a fairly well-rounded individual though like any of us, he was also human and faced difficult times where the heightened sensitivity needed for that intensely deep level of mediumistic work affected him – simply because he was almost electrified with spiritual energy.

In one memorable conversation we had, he shared thoughts about how difficult it was for him to accept some people who didn't possess the same passion he had for spirit communication and realise how incredibly sacred he felt it was. For a moment, he seemed despondent with the values many students had about such a wonderful spiritual gift as communication with those who had passed. For me, when Glyn was on form, he was one of the most evidential and dynamic mediums I'd ever seen demonstrating. Not only did he bring incredible evidence, but I could also feel the presence of those in the spirit world who were communicating with and through him. For Glyn never sounded like one of those mediums who brings what is almost like a formalised tick-list of evidence, during which I must admit to never feeling the presence of the spirit as I did with Glyn.

The gift of his presence, his teachings, and most valuable of all, he made me feel comfortable discussing subjects with him. He was, and still is, a well-known teacher. And me at that time? I was just a beginning student of mediumship. Yet Glyn treated me like an equal and not only allowed me to debate with him but encouraged me to voice my deepest thoughts, even if they were contrary to his own. What a *Gift* for a beginning student.

After knowing him for a few years, he invited me to visit

him in England. He took me to many wonderful places: to Oxford City, and to London to see a performance of Whirling Dervishes at London's Southbank. And, of course, we went to the best restaurants as Glyn always knew where to go for good food! I felt like I was a queen being entertained royally. To this day in my prayers I still send my thanks to Glyn for all the fun we had.

When Glyn became ill in 2003 with what was thought to possibly be Listeria (none of the doctors knew for sure what the illness was and what caused it), I was obviously upset and got in touch with him by phone to offer my support. When he was over the worst of it, he travelled to do both services and teach in the Boston area again. He confided in me that the illness and its effects had made life hard for him, but he still felt a deep need to keep working for spirit. My heart broke for him.

When news of Glyn's transition to spirit reached the Boston area, word spread quickly throughout the Spiritualist Churches Glyn had served on his trips to the US. Reverend Mary Di Giovanni scheduled a special memorial service at the Greater Boston Church of Spiritualism, and those of us who had known Glyn talked to the congregation about how much we had learned from him. This year a couple of my students who had studied with Glyn in seminars that he gave at Quincy Church, asked if we could study some of his teachings. This fall we have been focusing on the many things he taught us: the most important being the Sitting in the Power exercise that Glyn was so known for teaching. Many of us remember doing the exercise with Glyn and, believe me, it was not any ordinary meditation experience. His energy brought many of us to a new level in communication with the world of spirit.

Glyn will be remembered in the Boston area by all of us

who got to know him well during his many trips to the US. Thanks goes to Nancy Garber for making the arrangements for Glyn and to Reverend Rita Berkowitz who also hosted Glyn at her house. And in the years to come we will share our stories about Glyn and also his teachings with our students, including new ones who were never blessed to study with him. We thank Glyn for all that he gave us.

\* \* \*

### Some Treasured Memories
#### *by Janet Glasgow*

The first teaching weekend of Glyn's I attended was on one of his Gordon Higginson Fellowship weekends at the Seekers Trust in Addington, Kent. There must have been around 40 chairs set in a horseshoe shape in the main hall, which was literally buzzing with the energy of students' anticipation of what was to come; for they already knew what I would come to know very quickly!

I heard Glyn before I saw him – his rich loud and expressive voice cutting through the melee – then through the doors he came in wearing a lemon coloured short sleeved shirt and a walking stick that he used as an extension of his arm, waving it about and obviously happy to see us students and to be there.

What followed over the next two days was without exaggeration, life-changing for me and, I suspect, for many others who were present. As Glyn spoke to each of us there in turn, the genuine interest in his students was apparent. As was the effect of Glyn's voice, which felt as though he was always speaking to you directly and personally, even when he was speaking to the whole audience. For me, it seemed like Glyn knew that through the vibration of his voice, the power built and the influence of the spirit became stronger – it felt like all of us present knew this. He was a man whose wisdom, knowledge, humour and presence just kept on giving and giving.

I will never forget after Glyn had led us through the exercise Sitting in the Power that first morning, inwardly rejoicing that I had found someone in whom I could trust. That feeling never changed as we got to know each other well over the following years, and I am deeply blessed to have shared so many experiences with him. Like the one when Glyn was driving with Jean Dixon and me in his car near where he lived. We were driving through a country estate and the road suddenly became so full of cows that we had to stop. "Janet you'll have to get out and move them on", Glyn said. Not being a cow whisperer myself, I sheepishly got out and Jean came with me, who luckily and thanks to God it turned out, grew up on a farm and *is* a cow whisperer! Glyn sat impatiently waiting and telling us to hurry up while I was surrounded by angry cows who didn't want to move. Especially the head cow who had a major attitude, which Jean managed to save me from much to Glyn's amusement. He had such a way of saying "It will be alright" no matter what situation arose. And you could almost find yourself in any number of amusing situations with Glyn, but it was always "alright"!

His character was complex. He was highly sensitive to the vibration of different spiritual and psychic energies and knew when people were using them and what they might bring about. He would challenge and encourage you to challenge and encourage yourself to find balance in all things – to be a better person, friend and student, and to be kind to others.

Glyn was still working and teaching brilliantly to help students on a weekend course just five days before he passed and expressed his concern that he hadn't given students enough as he still had more he wanted to give. That was the measure of the man. He didn't just talk, he gave everything he had. Around that time, we spent several hours and journeys travelling by car to and from various places, and on various occasions, he would give a spontaneous sitting to either me or other passengers; the contents of which showed how truly gifted he was.

Glyn didn't often speak about his own experiences of things he'd witnessed in depth, but one evening at a restaurant in Torquay in Devon (we had to join a casino to get into the restaurant of which I think we are still members!), Glyn spoke about some of the amazing phenomena he'd witnessed in his life and the mediums through whom the phenomena had happened. Those of us who were lucky enough to be with him that night sat speechless listening to him. Of course, Glyn spoke many times about his great friend, mentor and the brilliant medium Gordon Higginson and Gordon's mother, Fanny, whom we felt we knew through Glyn's stories and teachings…wonderful!

Glyn, like many of us, had things he had to overcome in his life and, I believe, in his later life, he came to know what acceptance, forgiveness, compassion and love is really about. He taught it and embodied it. And boy did he earn it.

\* \* \*

## The Purple Silk Dress
### by Geoffrey Saunders

Both my parents died within months of each other when I was 17. I went to live with my mother's sister Alice. She sang in the church choir and encouraged my love of music.

At 22 I was accepted as a student of music at the RNCM (the Royal Northern College of Music). During my final year I was asked by my aunt's choir master to sing the baritone solos in their next performance of Handle's Messiah. Of course I was excited to be asked and I said yes. It was an important opportunity and I knew it would mean a great deal to my aunt also.

The day of the performance arrived, she put on a purple dress that she had bought especially for the occasion. She never asked if I was nervous or if I was in good voice, but in the hallway as we were leaving for the church, she looked at me directly and said, "Do you know what you are doing today?" I simply replied, "Yes I do". Happily all went well and we were both very proud.

I went on to work in musical theatres for another 20 years. Before she died she saw nearly all of my opening nights. I then joined the staff as a lecturer at the RNCM. In my first term, the staff were asked to attend a seminar held at Langdale Chase, a beautiful hotel in the Lake District. On the first evening I was sat at dinner with one of the singing teachers, international soprano Ava June. She told me she no longer sang professionally but sang sometimes at a Spiritualist church in London. She suggested that I might like to attend and talk to someone she knew visiting the church named Glyn Edwards. She thought he would be able to help me understand more. I decided to make an appointment to see him and several weeks later went on the train to London, not knowing what to expect.

I arrived at the address and introduced myself. Glyn put me at my ease immediately and took me into a pleasant sitting room, where we sat comfortably on either side of the fireplace. We chatted casually for a few minutes and then just as casually he asked, "Who is Alice?" I was so surprised, I said, "Oh my goodness, that's my Aunty Alice, my mother's sister". He said, "She is asking you directly, if you know what you are doing today". She is also showing me she is wearing a purple silk dress.

I had never told anyone about that day, or what she had said, in the beautiful purple dress bought for a very special important occasion because the Messiah was a big challenge for me. I remember being moved by her confidence in me, by not making a fuss, but simply trusting that if I said I knew what I was doing, that was all she needed to hear.

Glyn brought both my parents to our session and then other very significant people in my life, who have passed on. I shall always remember his kind manner and friendliness that afternoon.

\* \* \*

## Memories of a Beautiful Man
### by Jane Roberts

I first became aware of the medium Glyn Edwards when I began attending the Arthur Findlay College in Essex in 2006. I live in Australia but am fortunate to be able to visit my family who live in Gravesend in England, an hour's drive from the college, and half an hour from the Seekers Trust in Kent, where Glyn also ran courses. In that particular year, a family member was going through an incredibly bad time battling illness. I had been attending the Gravesend Spiritualist Church and was excited to hear that Glyn was to be one of the visiting mediums. I attended once again, on the night he was demonstrating, excited to say the least. I was struck by the gentle nature of the man I witnessed on the platform and when he came to me with a message that I could hardly believe...

He brought through my mum and nana, and told me that a spiritual journey was there for me to take – how the spirit were ready to help me to move forward and that Mum would always be there with me. He went on to tell me how much love and guidance was coming from the spirit and that the time was ripe for me to start my journey. I made some brief notes after the message and looked at what I had written later that evening. I considered it a great honour and felt very special to have received a message from a medium such as Glyn. During the illness of my relative and following his passing, I had daily listened to Glyn's double CD *Merging with Spirit Consciousness* whilst sitting in the Chapel of the hospital and then in my bedroom at my sister's home. It helped me to get through those very difficult days as well as allowed me to deepen my own spiritual awareness.

I then began to look at where Glyn might be teaching and to my delight, I discovered he did teaching weekends at the nearby Seekers Trust. Over the following few years, I attended weekends of his there whenever I visited my family in Gravesend. I remember always coming away from his courses in awe of the wonderful man that Glyn was and the connections to spirit that were always so natural and real on those weekends. It was immediately after one of them that Glyn had agreed to do a private sitting for me. He was not doing many due to health problems at the time. Once again, I felt honoured to be given information from spirit by Glyn. I always felt in awe of him, was always struck by his calm presence, and found him to be an amazingly knowledgeable man: he was both kind and wise. His mediumship always came across as humble and gentle.

When the allotted time was up for the sitting, Glyn turned to me and said, "My dear, I really have hold of your mother here. Would you mind if I continue as there is more that she wishes to speak about?" Of course, I gratefully replied, "Yes, please continue!" He must have been tired from the weekend of teaching and yet here he was working tirelessly for the spirit world, bringing so much confirmation and information from my spirit family. To this day he has been the only medium to bring me the true essence of my mum – such a precious gift. He gave me information from her that had never been spoken of before. Although I was aware of some details, I always felt there was more that I was not aware of. My mum passed suddenly at 58

Glyn reading while on holiday in Rome, at a cafe on the edge of St Peter's Square. Mid-September 2008.

years old. There was always a mystery as to my birth and my real father; it had remained a mystery at the time but with the help of both Glyn and the spirit world, I have amazingly now come to find my father's family.

During the sitting, there was also a lot of encouragement given to me to continue on my spiritual journey. He mentioned how the spirit world would help me as there was much that I will be doing. He said, "The spirit world are telling me, you will be doing things for them that you have never dreamed of. The spirit hold you in the palm of their hands".

I am eternally grateful for that particularly special hour with Glyn and that unique contact with the spirit. And yes, I am amazed at some of the work that is carried out with the spirit's guidance and inspiration, especially in the many areas of healing. Since that day, I have never placed a time limit on spirit when I have a client for a reading or healing appointment. It takes as long as spirit require! I will always remember Glyn with love for being the *beautiful man* who gave so much to so many.

\* \* \*

## A Deep and Long Friendship
*by Santoshan (Stephen Wollaston)*

The medium Gordon Higginson once told Glyn and me that we were destined to meet. Even Glyn's trance control Michael reassured me that we were meant to be friends when we first met, which was in the summer of 1989. I initially met Glyn at the foot of the main staircase at the Arthur Findlay College and we instantly hit it off and discovered plenty of common ground between us. He invited me on a course he was running about a month later at the college, on which he had booked, amongst others, a respected semi-retired Buddhist teacher and a Christian yogi. It was just what I was looking for, and also for Glyn it seemed, as we both came away at the end of his week with reams of notes and lists of wonderful books to read and jointly made our way to Watkins Books in central London – a popular watering hole for both of us – and filled up the boot of my car with various titles on mediumship, New Thought, mystical poetry, Buddhist psychology and Yogic wisdom. It was clear that we shared many similar interests and enjoyed drawing from more than one source for spiritual nourishment. One particular Yogic text Glyn often re-read and had various translations of and commentaries on, was Patanjali's *Yoga Sutra*, which interestingly includes not only the essential Eightfold Path of Yoga but a whole section on an array of psychic, mediumistic and miraculous powers that are often mentioned in the tradition.

*Glyn walking between two rows of trees at the Anjali Ashram (a Christian-Indian Ashram that combines aspects of both traditions in its rituals and teachings), Mysore, India. Late December 2009.*

Glyn frequently stayed at my place, as he not only enjoyed staying over and visiting London's bookshops but going to other venues such as the delightful East-West Shop in Covent Garden, which has sadly since closed, and going to classical concerts, plays, restaurants and the massive HMV music store that used to be on Oxford Street. On one occasion, he came in and sat on the sofa in my living room and instantly told me I had very recently been meditating on it. Incredibly, he was correct.

On another occasion we were travelling by taxi and noticed the driver taking peculiar routes to our destination instead of better roads that would have been more direct and less congested, so we decided to get out and walk. When we told the driver to stop, he suddenly became angry with us. I then got angry with him. As soon as Glyn and I were on the pavement, he asked me to take his hand as he wanted a bit of help to cross a busy main road but instantly shook my hand away and told me he could feel, just by briefly touching my hand, that I was still angry and I needed to let it go. He was right of course.

There were times when out of the blue he would tell me something was going to happen without any prior knowledge of a situation, such as winning a sum of £40 on a Premium Bond number he didn't previously know I had, and within three weeks it actually happened! Another time he told me I would get a new job where I would be greatly appreciated and this also came true. It occurred six months later when I started a new teaching post at a medical university in the Middle East for four years. I should mention here that from my experience in education, it's not usually common for management to be so grateful for the work teachers do, so Glyn's prediction can't be seen as merely guesswork.

Yet in spite of knowing Glyn so closely and for so long,

some might be surprised to read that I never had a sitting with him – though he did give me a message from my grandmother once during the Sunday Service at the Arthur Findlay College – as he already knew too much about me, though he'd always recommend a medium if I needed a sitting. I saw him work publicly many times of course, including working at some of the UK's largest public demonstrations of mediumship events, run by organisations such as the Spiritualists' National Union, Psychic News or people such as Jean Matheson, another long-time close friend of Glyn's.

The last time I saw Glyn working publicly was when he did an hour talk followed by questions and answers for the Positive Living Group in Glastonbury, in the summer of 2013. He started by mentioning people, practices and areas of unfoldment that meant something to him, such as New Thought teachings, the insights of Earnest Holmes (Glyn once did a week at the Arthur Findlay College *solely on* the Science of Mind teachings of Holmes), mediumship and its history, his understanding of the spirit world, Earth-centred spirituality, all life as being sacred, the Divine feminine verses masculine beliefs about God, the creativity of life, his times with Gordon Higginson and what he stood for, Buddhist Mindfulness, Centring Prayer, various yogis and Christian mystics and their experiences, contemporary psychology and scientific discoveries. He covered so much in his introduction that I began to wonder how his talk was going to make any sense at all! It turned out that I needn't have worried, as he awesomely brought everything together in an amazingly clear and synthesized whole. There were numerous times such as this when I, along with others, witnessed his brilliance.

We would both introduce each other to respected and

treasured friends from various paths and backgrounds. One of these was Bhikkhu Nagasena, who was an Indian Theravada Buddhist monk in his late 60s who lived nearby to me. I took Glyn to see him in the late summer of '99, as I knew they would instantly hit it off with each other. And they did! At first, Glyn wasn't sure whether to tell him that he was a known medium, but I suspected Nagasena wouldn't bat an eyelid as he simply enjoyed meeting people and wasn't interested in uninformed prejudices about different practices and paths. In fact Nagasena's response even surprised me, as the minute Glyn told him, Nagasena's eyes lit up and he enthusiastically responded by asking him, "Are you really? I used to subscribe to Psychic News! I'm very interested in healing". To which Glyn promptly invited him to be a day guest on his next course at the Arthur Findlay College as one of his fellow tutors was going to do healing workshops. Nagasena was more than pleased to accept the invite and arrived at the college wearing his traditional saffron monk's robes and had a marvellous time by all accounts. Plus the students loved meeting him, Glyn told me.

A few years later, Glyn and I became aware of Nagasena's health deteriorating and that he was living in a retirement home in a small room with very little warm clothing, bedding and furniture, such as an armchair. Glyn instantly announced this to students he was working with at the college and jointly put in and raised enough money to buy what Nagasena needed and personally delivered it to him within a few days, accompanied by two students who, along with Glyn, gave Nagasena some healing. I could of course continue mentioning plenty of other memorable times spent with Glyn and write more about his generous and compassionate nature, but I feel I ought to keep my recollections in this part of the book to roughly the same length as others'.

I trust that he is now enjoying his current spirit life in the same way he enjoyed much of his Earth life (though it should perhaps be mentioned that because of the omnipresence of the spirit world, that Glyn understood Earth life *as ultimately a spirit life*), surrounded by animal spirit friends, whose company he always cherished, and those of like minds to stimulate his passions for all things inclusive, universal and compassionately spiritual. Blessings to you Glyn.

*A very small piece of labradorite Glyn kept in his wallet. He bought it in a crystal shop in Glastonbury when we were there in 2013. He particularly liked it because the light picks up a lot of the shimmering blue in it. It is said to be an excellent crystal for strengthening one's energies and for awareness of our spirit Self, intuition and psychic abilities. Two and half years after Glyn's passing, I suddenly came across it in plain sight sitting on my kitchen floor, around the time I started to work on this book and just before coming down with a severe illness that took several months to overcome and stopped me from completing this anthology for a while. I've since considered the synchronistic discovery of this crystal to have been a message from Glyn and a way of him sending me some encouragement, and also healing through a difficult time.*

\* \* \*

## Shared Memories and Grateful Thanks
### by Mark Stone

Glyn was and is so many things to me, as he was and still is to many. He was my mentor, my favourite colleague to work alongside, and also a wonderfully supportive friend who cared deeply about me, my life, my spiritual journey and many of my students who he met over the years.

Although there are so many personal memories which will

always be held close and remembered in my heart, I would like to share the eulogy I wrote to read at the celebration of his life in June 2015, when so many people came together, spoke about him and shared their great love and appreciation of this truly unique man…

"We have returned to tell you, there is more to you, much, much more, so become the light and the beacon from which others light their own light, that they too may become a beacon." These were the words of Reamus, one of Glyn's guides speaking when I was with Glyn in Great Yarmouth shortly before his passing. I was lucky to have spent so many years with Glyn, at first as a student with him as my mentor, then for a short while as a gopher for him at the Arthur Findlay College, and then as our friendship continued to grow and develop, as a co-tutor and friend.

I met Glyn at a point in my life when I was ready to walk away from Spiritualism, and then, as the saying goes, "When the student is ready, the master appears", and he definitely was a master to me. He knew mediumship, lived mediumship, and certainly could demonstrate like no one else I had met. When I was at the college under his tuition, learning to understand what authentic mediumship encompassed, it often felt like I was being made to jump through hoops of fire through all the hours of the day and night. However, those were some of the happiest days of my life, and when some of my best friendships were established, including, of course, my friendship with Glyn.

After many years passed, Glyn would come to Bournemouth to work with me and my students at my own centre. Whenever he worked with students, he not only ignited their passion for the spirit world, but also their passion for their own mediumship and what might come of it. He cared greatly for them all and would often ask, when on the phone with me, how certain people were, how they were doing in their unfoldment, and always asked to be remembered to them. But how could anyone ever forget Glyn once they had met him?

When he came to visit, he would ask to go exploring in the lovely scenery of Dorset, to go out and find a nice place to amble around. Though interestingly, we always ended up somewhere mentioned in *The Good Food Guide*, as Glyn, like most of us, enjoyed good food. So, not only did I enjoy lovely walks around beautiful places with him, but some lovely memorable meals with wonderful conversation on all subjects of life – spiritual and mundane.

A few years ago, we went to a beautiful part of Dorchester where there was a working Friary and we spent many hours enjoying the scenery and spending time in the chapel in silent contemplation. I spoke to Glyn about the need we all have to be supported in our mediumship and how we should have retreats for us working mediums to support each other in our work. We talked about this at length, but as with so many ideas, life took over and we did nothing about it. That was until Glyn's diagnosis of cancer in 2014. Then one day he rang me and said, "Are you free on these dates as I have booked us into a retreat in a convent?" A number of us, including Glyn, had a wonderful weekend filled with laughter and camaraderie, discussing all aspects of our work, even our doubts and fears about the future of Spiritualism. Though being a group of Spiritualists on retreat in a convent, we could hardly let on to the nuns why we were there. But who do you think got cornered by one of the nuns and given the third degree about how we knew each other and why were we there? Yes, you guessed it, yours truly. I thought, "I can't lie to a nun", so some lovely creative and inspirational thinking came up about healing and praying for Glyn's health and sitting with the Holy Spirit. It was certainly a funny moment that we all laughed about later that night. However, out of that weekend came so much love, support, guidance and friendship that I will never forget.

On that weekend, which we were so lucky to have spent with Glyn, we also had the lovely Eric Hatton with us, who was one of the presidents of the Spiritualists' National Union, who came for a day to be with us and to share his views and reflections on Spiritualism today. When we spoke to him and asked for his advice regarding the future and what we could do, he said, "All I can tell you is to fight on!" And that is what we are doing, and what Glyn was doing, even in the face of the illness he was dealing with, he kept on teaching, kept on inspiring, and kept on caring. We spoke almost every day on the phone for many years, setting the world to rights and chatting about everything and anything. That support and friendship and being able to have a listening ear was a godsend for me.

We, who were lucky and privileged to have met him and worked with him, re-lit our lights and reignited our passion for mediumship because of him, will of course miss his physical presence and guidance in our lives. We hope to continue to share the light of his teachings and his memory to all those we meet on our spiritual pathways. Although those we meet and speak to may not have met Glyn in person, through us, we hope that his passion, teachings and humour will continue to touch and inspire them. For those of us who are mediums, we know there is no death. We know we will hear words of encouragement from Glyn again. And those of us who knew him and were inspired by him to teach and inspire others, have become the torchbearers of Glyn's work, just as he became one of the torchbearers of Gordon Higginson's work after Gordon passed to spirit.

It's sometimes the little things that mean so much... I had the great honour and pleasure of serving Paignton Spiritualist Church for their Easter Seminar weekend in 2017 along with my friend Sonia Driscoll, who also worked with Glyn. These seminars were started by Gordon Higginson many years before and countless wonderful mediums and teachers have continued to be a part of them ever since, including, of course, the marvellous Glyn. The 2017 Easter Seminar was on 31st March, which coincided with Hydesville Day, the birth of Modern Spiritualism. Because of this, I gave a talk on the Sunday morning about the pioneers of the movement and the importance of remembering and honouring our recent teachers and mentors, especially on seminars such as the ones at Paignton Church.

I spoke of many happy memories of the bank holiday seminars at Paignton and one particular one with Glyn, Jill Harland and Muriel Tennant I had attended nearly 15 years earlier. It was especially powerful and moving for me in many ways. Not only for the teachings I and others received from three exceptional mediums, but also for privately spending some wonderful time with them. Then just before the evening service, a steward ran to me and handed me a piece of folded paper and told me that it had just fallen out of one of the hymn books she had been handing out in the church (books used hundreds, if not thousands, of times since the seminar I spoke of). I looked at it and saw it was in fact a flyer about the very same seminar with Glyn, Muriel and Jill! It had been held in the pages of a hymn book for so long and could have fallen out and been discarded years ago, but here it was on this particular day.

I was surprised, elated, emotionally moved and, most of all, comforted to know that these three wonderful mediums I knew and loved, but now in spirit, had been with us throughout the seminar and had clearly made their presence known. For me, it's sometimes in the small things that I find great confirmation of those in spirit letting me know they are still with me. I now keep that flyer in my suit pocket to remind me of those who not only played a part in my unfoldment years ago but also now.

\* \* \*

## Glyn at Longton Spiritualist Church
*by Kathryn Shirley*

As the current president of Longton Spiritualist Church, I would like to share the following treasured memories about Glyn.

Longton Church was the church and hometown of the great Gordon M Higginson, who during his lifelong involvement

*Glyn in East London. Taken in the late summer of 1989. The photo was used for the covers of Glyn's first series of recordings on mediumship in the early 90s.*

within mediumship and Spiritualism, occasionally took young mediums under his wing. Glyn was one such medium who Gordon saw great potential in and not only supported and encouraged him, but also the two of them became close friends, and enjoyed many social times outside of meetings, services and teaching together. In particular, they went on holidays with each other, along with their mutual friends Jean Matheson and Santoshan.

Glyn was a firm favourite when he took services at Longton Church and would always attract a crowd. After the passing of Gordon in January 1993, the old church was closed, and a little over a year after moving into a temporary building, the new one opened in 1995 with a special celebration. Glyn was often invited to be a part of the church's workshop weekends, which were organised by the medium Paul Jacobs (the president of the church at the time) and the church committee. This would have been around 1996. During one of those weekends, Glyn took the Sunday Divine Service, which begins at 6:30pm and ends at 7:45pm. Glyn began his address at approximately 6.45pm and captured the attention of the congregation for a full 45 minutes. He was never one to be conventional, walked off the platform (unheard of!) and touched people's shoulders as he strolled down the aisle and back again. After a while, the chairperson discreetly informed Glyn that the service usually ends around 7:45 and he would only have 10 minutes left to demonstrate. Undeterred and in full flow, Glyn responded, "That's as maybe my dear, but I shall continue until I have finished". He held the congregation of approximately 80 in the palm of his hands and not one of them left until he said he had finished! That service ended at around 8:15pm and if the congregation had their way, it would have continued; for the passion and joy which emanated from Glyn was exceptional, and all who enjoyed that evening were swept along with the flow just as much as Glyn was. What a wonderful orator he was. You could not help but feel inspired by him.

A second encounter with Glyn was during my only stay at the Arthur Findlay College, where I was placed in Glyn's development group. Every morning he began the day's learning by taking the students through the exercise of Sitting in the Power, an exercise that I continue to use. Listening to Glyn's melodic tones was not a difficult discipline to complete. And again, his passion and love of the spirit world shone through! At the end of each session, he would leave the room to spend time with his guide "Nicotina", as he used to smoke back then but quit later in his life, in order for him to gather his thoughts and take a break from us students.

On the Wednesday evening, he took part in the evening demonstration of mediumship, along with Paul Jacobs. It was explained that both of them would be taking part in an experiment, and that Glyn would begin. He turned his back to the Sanctuary congregation, with a microphone in his hand and began to blend with the spirit world. He started the link by stating, "I have a lady here who is someone's Granny Smith and was a widow for more years than she was with her husband". Paul then asked for a show of hands – only I understood this, as indeed my maiden name is Smith, and so I had a Granny Smith, who was widowed in her 50s and lived until she was 93 years of age. It was an outstanding demonstration. One that has stayed with me for 24 years.

Glyn is remembered for being flamboyant, passionate, kind, generous and loving, and he is still spoken about at Longton, where his memory will remain a testament to the man he was.

\* \* \*

## Spirit Ambassador
### by Micky Havelock

I was lucky to have Glyn as one of my first ever tutors at the Arthur Findlay College, for which I will always be grateful. His passion, dedication and discipline were great examples of the requirements to be an ambassador for spirit. I continued to study with him whenever the opportunity allowed for many years. His passion could sometimes make you quiver with nervousness as it would sometimes get the better of him and his enthusiasm would bubble over and his voice would dynamically display this. He could see your potential. And when you doubted yourself or were lazy with your own discipline, Glyn would always know. He was one of the students' biggest champions and only ever wanted the best for everyone and the spirit world. I loved his encouragement and I have to say I loved his passion and no-nonsense approach.

Through Glyn, I had my first ever experience of a trance demonstration. I was young and nervous and not sure what to expect. The muscles on the left side of Glyn's face had weakened after a mystery illness he had in 2003. As the doors were locked and the trance began, I was in awe as I watched his face lift and change for the hour he allowed spirit to talk through him. I remember blinking hard several times, testing that I was really seeing the changes to his facial features and left-hand side disfigurement. The wisdom that was shared was both moving and inspiring. The energy in the room was palpable and with the change to his face, the whole experience was captivating. The spirit communicator explained how they were working through him, and while they were doing this, they were giving him healing. For an hour, the audience sat still and silently drank in the inspiring wisdom of the spirit. As they began to withdraw, it was clearly visible that Glyn's face had immediately returned to how it was before. I walked the grounds of the college after processing the phenomena I had just witnessed. The trust he had in allowing spirit to work through him in that way and the total surrender it took for him to step aside to allow spirit to speak was truly amazing.

In-between classes I would often see Glyn walking around the grounds at the college, hands behind his back, deep in thought or if he had company, deep in conversation. He always astounded me with the knowledge he had on so many spiritual topics. There was always so much to learn from listening to his lectures on spirituality, mediumship and the interactive spirit world. He had studied so many religions and always seemed so curious about the wonders of life and the spirit. He had so many amazing memories of working with such great ambassadors of the spirit that had since passed and would often recount stories about them with laughter, warmth and a very obvious sense of respect for them. He openly shared lessons he had learned in his own development and struggles. I found him to be truly inspiring. It is because of him that I learnt the importance of Sitting in the Power for both individual and spiritual unfoldment. His inclusion of the exercise was always a big part of his workshops and courses.

I took my sceptical (at the time) husband along to one of Glyn's demonstrations. He came to my husband and delivered intricate details about my husband's grandfather, such as his name and the places he lived and worked. He also conveyed his personality along with many memories my husband and his grandfather shared. I was excited that my husband was having such a powerful experience of spirit communication. He sat there stunned. Several times I had to answer for him as he was lost for words. The depth of the information, lots of which I was not aware of and the ease at which Glyn delivered it left my husband in no doubt that his grandfather was communicating from the spirit world. To witness first-hand the effect that quality of mediumship can have on someone was really inspiring. Glyn had passed on such detailed information with such ease that it touched my husband in very deep ways. Afterwards, my husband left the demonstration and was no longer a sceptic but curious and open-minded.

Occasionally, when I'm doing the Sitting in the Power exercise, I feel Glyn draw close. It is not a regular occurrence, but when he pops by, I feel a change happening to my facial features, along with Glyn's energy and encouragement. It is comforting to know he still likes to check up on my progress. He would always push me for more – that soft encouragement of his coupled with his passion, drive and the objective observations he often gave.

His passion was infectious. He used to get so enthusiastic about others' progress and achievements, and would sometimes proudly ask us students if we had seen what others had achieved and the marvellous things they were doing. This was Glyn, how I saw him, such a complex man with a big heart and *sometimes* a bit of a temper to match. There are so many memories I am lucky to have had with him. These are just a few of them. I will forever be grateful for his encouragement and support for my own development and I miss the laughter and wisdom he readily shared. I miss his passion, dynamic public voice and physical presence. Glyn was one of a kind: unique, gifted, inspirational and dedicated to the spirit world of which he is now residing.

\* \* \*

PART TWO

# *Selection of* Teachings & Reflections *by* Glyn Edwards

ARTICLES, QUOTATIONS, EXERCISES
AND WORKSHOP SECTIONS

## Quotations by Glyn Edwards

*For me, mediumship is not just a gift or an ability
but a sacred vocation.*
*~ The Potential of Mediumship (expanded edition)*

\* \* \*

*The highest principle in all life is the spirit
and it is this which gives life to physical form.*
*~ The Spirit World in Plain English*

\* \* \*

*Ultimately, mediumistic and spiritual unfoldment are
active and evolving paths that lead to new and
profound experience and deep communion
with the world of the spirit.*
*~ The Spirit World in Plain English*

\* \* \*

*We need to recognise that there are different ways in which to
approach the many faceted dimensions of spirituality and be
open to numerous areas that can lead us to healthier states of
spiritual being and embrace the all-ness of
what eternal life is about.*
*~ Realms of Wondrous Gifts*

\* \* \*

*All we need to do is be responsive to positive growth and
willing to be more active instruments for the compassionate
and creative work of the spirit.*
*~ The Spirit World in Plain English*

\* \* \*

# 2
# Intuitive Arts

*This article was put together by Glyn for the Gordon Higginson Fellowship website in 2006 and includes a workshop section designed by him in 2013. Extracts from the article were later used in 'The Potential of Mediumship' anthology of his wisdom. This and the following chapter beautifully capture Glyn's deep passion for a universal and holistic approach to spirituality and mediumship.*

Psychic and mediumistic powers have manifested in many of the inspiring spiritual traditions of both the East and West. They have been experienced in numerous mystical and spiritual states and stages of awareness and are common to many people. Powers that we call psychic have no boundaries, whether they manifest mediumistically, artistically or as pure intuition. They exist in an infinite variety of forms and can possess great value in the different ways they manifest.

The intuitive self, the knower that knows the unknown, the shaman that sees into the vision quest, the yogi that develops the *siddhis* (miraculous powers), the seer that sees into the possible, the sensitive who has the ability to communicate with many levels of life and with those that we love, will all come to discover there are no limitations to the numerous powers they possess. They are all facets of our true spirit Self. Even the power of creative thought, which can bring communities together, is in many respects one of the greatest gifts. Yet all powers ultimately interconnect and can influence one another in numerous creative ways.

The artist that paints, expresses psychic impressions within herself by what she sees, hears or feels. The orator, the poet and the teacher uses her creative powers in numerous levels of expression that draw upon intuitive psychic skills. The word psychic comes from the Greek word *psyche*, which dictionaries describe as soul/personality, mind/consciousness/mental processes, and spirit/innermost being, and sometimes define it as the breath of life. It is a part of ourselves that is invisible but nonetheless real.

In the first coauthored book I did with Santoshan, we pointed out how we can know nothing of physical life if it were not for our psychic senses, as everything we perceive is processed through them. Every day of our physical existence, we encounter and experience psychic impressions and relate to daily life through them in the different ways we think, speak and act. We experience everything in symbolic form, which has symbolic meaning to us, including language and all other sensory data. Our mind and conscious awareness perceive all things as psychic images, sensations, energies and vibrations, which then influence us and express themselves in and through our being. Whether we realise it or not, we daily live in a psychic world, and creative and mediumistic abilities interconnect with this, as well as with transforming realms of spirituality. It is by healthily awakening to the various forces within our life that all areas of existence become integral parts of a spiritual whole.

## Worlds within Worlds

The worldwide interest we see happening into realms of psi-phenomena, prophecy, seership, mediumship and spirituality show a growing thirst for something more than just egocentric existence. All these things are filled with creative potential, transforming wisdom and infinite possibilities.

We can look to these areas of ability and understanding as entrances to invisible worlds that can lead us to realised knowledge and different ways of being. They are not worlds of entertainment or about escapism but facets of being that can be both life affirming and transforming. They are about discoveries of inner powers that open us to our true purpose and a profound understanding of life's deepest mysteries. They show us that we are more than just our bodies – that our individual being and consciousness are facets of an essential spiritual Source.

This obviously is not a denial of crucial spiritual gifts we possess such as our compassionate nature or reflective and healthy reasoning abilities. But we need to be careful of following paths that focus *solely* on the heart, without including wisdom and flexible contemplative states of mind. For when the heart and mind are in balance with one another, the reflective, reasoning and wise parts of ourself can be used to *healthily* expand our understand of life. They are integral parts of spiritual growth, just as much as compassion is, and link with intuitive states of knowing.

All of our abilities need to be included and harmonised with one another in order to establish authentic stages of wholeness and unfoldment. We physically exist because of our spiritual origins. The spirit seeks to express itself through our body, mind and feelings in order to influence and harmonise all that we do and are. There is no end to our evolvement and the potential within us. It is only we who limit ourselves with inhibiting beliefs about our spiritual nature and inherent gifts.

When we focus on and work with our inner abilities, we

unfold mediumistic powers and the vision of the seer and the prophet. Nothing then remains hidden or unknown. We allow our growth to unfold naturally and become aware of our own authentic spirit and the many levels of divinity and creativity that exist, including the ability to communicate with spirit helpers who connect with numerous realms of existence. And when we awaken to these realms, we come to realise how all things exist in the Divine and the spirit world, and how they are profoundly interwoven.

If we are open to allowing it, this awakening can influence us in daily life, lead us to discovering our finest qualities and to realising that life never dies; it only changes its state and is eternal. Ultimately, unfoldment leads us to our authentic Nature, which has been interpreted in different ways by different traditions: as spirit, *sat-chit-ananda* (pure being, consciousness and bliss), original goodness, the Divine Self, and our Buddha Nature. Through searching we come to ask the age-old questions: "Who am I?", "What am I?", "Why am I here?", "Where am I going?" and "What is creating the appearance of separation from my authentic spiritual nature?" Such questions lead us to a discovery of our greatest qualities of love, compassion, kindness and unity with all things, life, people and species. For if all is interrelated, we cannot consider the suffering of others as being separate from ourselves.

Do you have the courage to awaken to and live this radical vision and the truth that can set you free? Spiritual empowerment is in the discovery of who we truly are, which includes the deepest implications for spiritual living. Our spirit knows the means of expressing the light of our authentic being. We only need to listen to its call and be inspired by its profound influence.

\* \* \*

## Guidance of the Spirit
### Workshop Reflection

Much is misunderstood about spirit guidance. We need to consider that we are dealing with a spirit world that consists of individuals who are naturally intelligent. Their presence and purpose is to guide and influence us to the original and greater good of ourselves, and to reflect upon how we can live our lives in wholesome ways.

Those in the spirit world, like us, have undergone human experience and know of the difficulties of human life. The purpose of their coming to work with you is to enhance, enrich and expand the vision of your life. The spirit seeks to encourage you to honour yourself, all life, and the universal Divine Spirit in all. They seek to encourage you to:

- Find spiritual enrichment in your life and awareness.
- Enhance your abilities to love others and yourself, and unfold qualities of wisdom and kindness.
- Empathise with and feel compassion for all life and be aware that this does not just mean *human* life.
- Cultivate an interlinked physical, spiritual and ethical life.
- Honour people's rights to think and act according to the spiritual paths they have chosen.
- Rise above judgmental thoughts and restrictive projections that separate you from others, as ultimately there are no "others" as we are all interconnected in the oneness of spirit.

These things, when healthily and wholesomely applied, will enhance your mediumistic unfoldment, and the numerous qualities and areas of your spiritual nature and everyday awareness.

## Quotations by Glyn Edwards

*Anything that separates us from others means separating ourselves from life and the awe inspiring creativity of God and spirit working through all.*
*~ Spirit Gems*

\* \* \*

*All life is sacred and ultimately derives its existence from God. We therefore need to seek to become one with this sacredness that exists in everything and everyone and respect and care for all life, including ourselves.*
*~ Spirit Gems*

\* \* \*

*Life on Mother Earth is not a negative place that we feel we would be only too pleased to escape. Her beauty inspires awe and wonder and has great healing qualities.*
*~ Realms of Wondrous Gifts*

\* \* \*

*Behind all there is that which is creative, the same Spirit in all, which has imbued all life with the ability to express its creativity, to become co-creators, and has allowed humanity to discover life's true purpose and meaning – that ultimately everything is ruled by love and that our true nature is ultimately loving.*
*~ Realms of Wondrous Gifts*

\* \* \*

# 3
# Varieties of Unfolding Mediumistic Experience

*A previously unfinished article Glyn started in 2009, with extra material from remembered conversations with him added to complete it. It includes two workshop sections designed by Glyn in 2013.*

Some reflections I wish to share for this article are drawn from my experiences as a medium, along with many years of inquiry into various spiritual practices, insights, teachings and experiences other people have had.

I have seen spirit people since I was a child and did my first public demonstration of mediumship when I was 19. At an early age, I encountered different experiences that could be classed as having a psychic element to them. At the age of 16, I entered a Christian monastery and started to follow the monastic community's regular practices of prayer, reflection and meditation, and noticed that the early experiences I had been having were beginning to intensify because of the practices I was doing. The reason for mentioning the latter, is because other people I know such as the Yoga master Swami Dharmananda Saraswati Maharaj and some of her students have also found similar things happening to them. Yet for them, it was not, of course, because of Christian monastic practices bringing the experiences about but various Yoga practices. Swamiji herself once told me that she was not in fact focusing on or even considering awakening experiences or abilities that could be classed as being of either a mediumistic or psychic nature at the time. And for some of her students, this has also been the case.

A young and charming English Swami I once met and spoke to some years ago at the tranquil Ramakrishna Vedanta Centre in Bourne End, in England, mentioned to me that after becoming a monk and doing regular practices of Yogic meditation and mantra, he started to develop some of the classic Yogic and Buddhist powers mentioned in an array of Indian scriptures, particularly one that is often described as the "divine ear" and associated with a unique ability to be aware of the cries of all carnate and discarnate creatures both nearby and at a great distance. It is in fact a power that displays a profound opening to the suffering of others – to humans and other beings and species' suffering. The young swami mentioned how at first, he had found it difficult to handle and how, once again, it was not something he was expecting or even trying to unfold in his spiritual life and practices.

### A Natural Part of Our Being

I feel it is important that we embrace the light that is there in numerous spiritual traditions, and realise that nationality, spiritual background or beliefs have nothing to do with the phenomena of mediumistic and psychic powers, as they are a natural part of everyone's being and found manifesting in the majority, if not all, of the world's great wisdom and mystical traditions. And, as shown in the previous examples, these powers can manifest without consciously trying to unfold them. Although, it should perhaps be mentioned here, our beliefs may colour our perceptions and understanding of them. Our prevalent state of awareness and any concepts we hold can condition the emergence of any mediumistic or psychic abilities because of them working through the mechanisms of our finite physical mind, body and feelings. It is therefore helpful to look at ourselves, our beliefs and our perceptions, and see how we can be more openly receptive to the world of the spirit, and mindfully aware of those that may work with us from that interconnected realm, which is also a part of us. For we ourselves are spirit in physical form.

Like me, there are others who have had or displayed mediumistic and psychic abilities from an early age but, as mentioned earlier, there are others who have not. They came about later in life and only after undertaking practices that were not specifically performed for the purpose of unfolding them. I make this point as there are *some*, and I emphasise the word "some", who believe that mediumship is something that distinctly shows itself early in life and only manifests within the Spiritualist movement or a selected few who were uniquely born with the ability.

As is often the case, there are numerous areas to consider when it comes to spiritual practices and mediumistic powers. For me, I feel we need to be careful when it comes to considering any single perspective or single person as having the whole subject sewn up. I mention this as I sometimes come across students wishing to promote an authority figure as having *the final say on everything*, and anyone contradicting what that person teaches is jumped upon as being misguided or misinformed. This can disempower us and undervalue trust in our own natural wisdom, our own personal experiences and insights into unfoldment, and is in fact psychologically harmful and spiritually inhibiting. It can cause distrust in any spiritual guidance we have received up to that point and may have been following.

The subject of mediumistic and psychic powers is, in fact, multifaceted. Including, that when we talk to another person in the physical world we are in fact communicating with another spirit personality because of the spirit that exists in all people, species and things. So, in a way, if we embrace this understanding, our everyday interactions with life can be viewed as a form of mediumship.

I once received a letter from someone who wrote to me about a particular medium's teachings she had been following. She wanted to put forward the teachings as being the last word on any discussion about mediumship and my understanding of it being a perfectly natural and integral part of everyone (although many may not actually realise it). She mentioned how the medium she followed taught about mediumship being an *abnormality* and how people either had it or did not.

From my own experience, I do not consider mediumship to be abnormal and wonder what is being implied by the use of the word. What measuring stick is being used to define normal, let alone abnormal? For me, the term has a derogatory tone to it and does not sound like the right word to use. I have never thought of my mediumistic life as being abnormal but as an inherent part of my being. And traditions such as Yoga, which have been around for much longer than modern-day Spiritualism, have never used the term to describe psychic powers or classified mediumistic abilities such as clairvoyance, clairaudience or clairsentience as abnormal, although various yogis and great wisdom teachers of the past often focused on other realms of unfoldment. For instance, although the historical Buddha knew that practices of meditation could lead to psychic abilities and even used them in his life and the night of his enlightenment, the bulk of his teachings are on practical everyday living, compassion, overcoming unsatisfactoriness and suffering, and establishing sublime states and stages of peacefulness and liberation.

## Approaching Contradictions with Maturity

If we consider how it is not uncommon to hear about one spirit guide or teacher saying one thing and another saying the complete opposite, we soon realise it is important for us to develop our own reflective reasoning and insights about spirituality and mediumistic unfoldment. These are after all important things to include in healthy spiritual growth.

If we are realistic about development, we will accept that people are sharing views based on their own personal experiences, knowledge and understanding, along with teachings they may have come to accept in their lives. And how these are interpreted can vary from one person to another. Hopefully, we will honour others and maturely agree to disagree with those holding different perspectives to our own. Spiritual maturity is an essential part of wholesome and skilful growth that needs to be included in our development if we truly wish to progress and move forward in harmony with others.

Some of the early trance controls of mediums such as JJ Morse (see his book *Practical Occultism*) pointed out that the underlying aim of the spirit's work, their teachings and messages, is to encourage us to develop ourselves in healthy ways and to seek the wisdom that is *within us*, rather than looking to spirit communicators and teachers for guidance and answers on *all* matters. To me, this clearly fits with two of Spiritualism's key principles: Personal Responsibility and Eternal Progress.

Traditions such as Buddhism, Hinduism and Christianity have recognised certain practices that can awaken followers to powers that can be classed as mediumistic in their nature, such as the "divine ear", as previously mentioned, and the "divine eye" (terms used in both the Buddhist and Hindu Yoga traditions). Even within scientific fields, there are people such as the Cambridge biologist Rupert Sheldrake who have recognised powers and memories that can be classed as psychic embedded within the workings of Nature, of which we are a part, and in the habits of various species. Sheldrake's discoveries have highlighted a collective interconnected consciousness that goes beyond individual physical realms of interaction and knowing.

==I feel that those of us who might class ourselves as mediums have to be cautious of seeing ourselves as different from others. Everyone has an individual uniqueness of course, but to see oneself as more unique or special than other people is problematic and grounded in egocentricness.== Signs of an authentic spirituality, on the other hand, are found in teachings of inclusiveness, equality, acts of compassion, and honouring different beliefs, insights, practices, ethnicity, sexual orientation and gender. If we embrace mediumship along with unitive perspectives that look for the best in all of us, they may ultimately guide us to seeing everyone as mediumistic in one way or another and as a member of our global family because of our shared origins and everyone's ability to be aware of the *universal* Spirit in physical form. In various traditions this understanding is described in different ways: in Buddhism as recognising ever-present Buddha Nature; in Judaism as *ruach*, the spirit and the breath of life; in Hinduism as the *atman*, the spark of divinity in all; and in Christianity as the Divine indwelling and the Cosmic Christ.

We see from this that there are numerous realms to consider and the possibility of an array of life affirming perspectives we could embrace. It is of course up to each and every one of us to consider where we individually stand and whether we maturely accept that no matter what position we may take, there will always be those with different views to our own, with valid points and insights to consider. Ultimately, all we need to do is learn how to be comfortable with this multifaceted diversity of understanding, be comfortable in our own skin, and find mutually beneficial ways in which we can live in harmony with our global sisters and brothers and discover a profound and sacred unity in the enriching realms of spiritual and mediumistic awakening.

\* \* \*

### Patterns of Mediumistic Experience
### Workshop Reflection

In mediumistic unfoldment, experiences will manifest indicating recognisable patterns in your growth. They are often broad in their spectrum and can be noticed running throughout the whole of mediumistic experience – through the beginnings of unfoldment and numerous essential areas. Crucial practices that interlink with these patterns, which can help you to be more aware of them in your development, are:

- Allowing for the unfoldment of self-awareness.
- Allowing yourself to accept experiences with an "Is it true?" questioning mind.
- Allowing your mind to be openly objective for mediumistic experiences to prove their reality.
- Allowing for a stillness and harmony of the mind and body.
- Allowing for receptiveness towards any experiences and embracing them.
- Allowing yourself to be open to changes and any transforming experiences that affect your mind, body and feelings.
- Allowing yourself to realise that unfoldment is a living interrelationship with all.
- Allowing yourself to foster openness, awareness and oneness in all areas of your life.

## Beliefs and Believing
### Workshop Reflection

Because of our belief in life after death as a provable fact (and we must stress *provable* beyond reasonable doubt), as developing mediums we need to promote within ourselves a healthy and mature attitude towards beliefs that others may hold. We must be careful of any idea we have about others needing to adopt the same beliefs as our own, but instead make allowances for the variety, diversity and richness of different paths. We need to take into consideration that others could inform us with conviction based on both experience and insight that their beliefs have deep levels of truth to them that have authentically enriched their lives. Therefore, accepting a diversity of paths that lead to the spirit is important to cultivate. The following are some thoughts for consideration:

- Honouring other paths enables you to honour your own and earn the respect of others.
- If someone disrespects the path you have chosen, you do not need to take it to heart or justify yourself, but honour what you believe and know to be true and bless the person for sharing his/her thoughts and being open with you.
- Be mindful of holding too tightly onto differences of opinion that divide and separate you from honouring all people and life.
- In order to embrace beliefs that are more thought-through, realise that Truth can never be neatly sewn up to any single belief – there will always be areas of contradiction which will require reflecting upon and awakening to your own insights.
- Allow room for mature growth, wisdom, paradox and the mystery of the unknown, as these will always encourage healthy and wholesome growth.

## Quotations by Glyn Edwards

*Spirit communication seeks to prove to humanity that all life survives death. It seeks to encourage us to reflect upon life, upon our beliefs and actions and take responsibility for the evolution of our spiritual nature.*
~ The Potential of Mediumship

\* \* \*

*Unfoldment is really about an ongoing discovery of the spirit world, consciously seeking help from the spirit, how to creatively co-operate with them, and realising how our unfoldment can enhance any abilities we have.*
~ The Potential of Mediumship (expanded edition)

\* \* \*

*As we develop a deeper response to and understanding of our sensitivity and spiritual and psychic nature, we allow the spirit's presence to manifest more fully in our lives and guide us onto richer planes of being and consciousness.*
~ Spirit Gems

\* \* \*

*Life is always about moving on and evolving in the eternity of existence, and each of us needs to face each moment, each passing phase of life with wisdom, acceptance and compassionate understanding.*
~ The Potential of Mediumship

\* \* \*

# Quotations by Glyn Edwards

*Through mediumistic experience we discover knowledge of another life from which we came and to which we will return.*
*~ The Potential of Mediumship*

\* \* \*

*Our beginning-less and endless Self does not need to view life as missed opportunities but seeks to call us to ways in which it can skilfully manifest its true nature, its divinity, more purely in every moment.*
*~ Realms of Wondrous Gifts*

\* \* \*

*If we look at the early years of modern Spiritualism, we find accounts of spirit communicators bringing not only messages about continuous human progression and survival but also seeking to encourage a recognition of the profound unity we have with all people and all life.*
*~ The Potential of Mediumship (expanded edition)*

\* \* \*

*An authentic trust in the spirit is about embracing the beginning of a deep friendship between yourself and the invisible world of those that work with you. This trust is an evolving experience that builds over time and through the experiences you undergo. But the most important ingredient of trust, is trust in yourself and your abilities.*
*~ The Potential of Mediumship*

\* \* \*

# 4

# Meetings with a Yoga Master

*Glyn shared the following amazing account of several meetings with a Yoga master at the request of Psychic News, who ran it as a two-part feature in 2013.*

Some years ago, a friend and I made our way down a dirt track alley in the back streets of Ilford in East London, and climbed up a rusty old weatherworn iron staircase in order to enter what we were told by respected Indian friends of ours was a place where we would meet a renowned Indian Tantric Yoga master.

As we got to the top of the staircase, there was an open wooden door that led to an unlit narrow corridor and plainly decorated back room, situated above a Cash and Carry shop, with chairs placed around it. But there was no sign to tell us we were in the right place and no other people to be seen, though we could hear some people talking in an adjacent room. We began to wonder if we had unintentionally walked into the wrong house and were about to give some people a bit of a shock when they saw us standing in their living room. However, our concerns were soon put to rest when an elderly, slightly-built, short bald-headed Indian gentleman appeared from the next room and asked us to following him. It turned out he was an interpreter for the man we had come to see. Although the person we were seeking could speak some English, the interpreter, along with other Hindi speakers who visited the centre, often helped translate more complex information.

My friend and I were both led into the room from where we had just heard voices speaking and were asked to take a seat on the floor in front of another sprightly looking Indian gentleman who was sitting crossed-legged on a low sofa in front of us. As we looked at him, we both couldn't help noticing his piercing eyes. Even though we found out later he was in his 80s, his eyes were sharp and penetrating, and his physical presence emanated a tangible energy that lifted our spirits just by being in the room with him.

He had been recommended to us as a person we should seek out. Apart from this, we had been told very little else about him, other than he came to Ilford twice a year from his native town, Jammu, which he was named after. We later found out he was actually highly respected, and that people from all backgrounds, including Indian politicians and famous people such as our Indian friends, who were known singers, sought audiences with him and would ask for guidance on numerous matters, domestic and spiritual. We also got to hear about people who would travel from the other side of the country in England, and how the same happened in India, in order to spend just a few brief minutes with him.

As soon as we sat down, the interpreter looked at a piece of yellow paper that Jammu had quickly written on, which amazingly explained why my friend and I had gone to see him. He looked at me with great warmth and told me the reason I had sought his advice was because of experiences of light I was having. He was absolutely correct and began to explain exactly what was happening and what I needed to do to take these experiences forward. He also mentioned various changes that were taking place with me and what would happen through various experiences I would encounter in the future.

He then turned his attention to my friend and gave him advice about his development. He then held out a stick about the size of a normal walking stick, which he placed at the point between our eyebrows, popularly called the "third eye", said some quiet mantras while doing this and told us that what he had done had aided the energy and power of our spiritual awareness.

He then asked us to describe what we had seen and/or experienced during this time and seemed satisfied with our answers. After that, he gave us instructions about *mudras* (hand gestures that can be used in meditation), mantras and visualisations to practice, which we later found beneficial, and asked us to come back in three days and report any experiences that had unfolded. It was at this point in the meeting that my attention was drawn to a point between Jammu's right thumb and forefinger, as there began to appear, though not yet solid or fully formed, a large date fruit, which he then gave to me and told me to eat later. When I did, I found it affected my awareness in a way that even now is hard to explain.

After this first meeting, my friend and I regularly went to see Jammu every time he came to England, and saw him on a number of occasions. Every time we met, he would materialise something such as sweets or herbal remedies if we were not feeling well, which we would be instructed to place in water and drink over a period of days. These things always had a positive effect, I found.

He would always know the purpose of our visits and the exact time we had left our homes in order to see him. He seemed to know our thoughts and struggles. He always gave us an answer to or guidance on questions or difficulties we had.

One of the things I remember him saying to me was never to doubt myself, to have confidence and self-trust. He told me this at a time when I was going through a bad-patch and was particularly lacking self-trust. The minute I entered the room, he told me all about this problem and waved a gentle finger while admonishing me in a friendly and caring manner to never let this attitude of mind affect me again, but to love and trust myself because I was God's child and God loved me, just as God loved all of his/her creations.

Every time my friend and I visited him, *dharshan* (a blessing) was given. He would always ask about things we had experienced. Sometimes, when he asked us to sit in front of him and meditate for a short period and asked what we had experienced, and was not satisfied with the result, he would ask us to sit again until a certain experience was noticed by us, such as a particular sound, feeling of energy or a mental image.

On each visit, he would give, and often materialise, *prasad* (blessed food), which is deemed as a spiritual gift, which he would often ask us to eat there and then. We frequently tried to leave him some money for his time, but more often than not, he refused to take it and gave it back, saying there was no need as we were now his family. Before leaving, he would always instruct his son and daughter-in-law to make us coffee or Masala tea and give us something to eat. Over time we became extremely close to both him and his family.

I sometimes took mediums and students I had been working with at the Arthur Findlay College to see him, and my friend sometimes took people he knew. Yet it was interesting to see how some found meeting a man from a different tradition to their own didn't always click with them, as not everyone was able to comprehend what he was about. People who did have an understanding of his lineage and tradition did however recognise what he stood for. He had many experiences relating to the spirit world and saw all things as parts of a Divine spiritual whole. I once asked him how some of the phenomena witnessed by many that went to him were possible. "God, the spirit and the light makes all this possible", he replied.

One significant event occurred after my friend and I introduced a female Yoga teacher, Swami Darhmananda Saraswati, to him, who used to teach at the Arthur Findlay College. They instantly took to and recognised something special in each other. After a few visits, Jammu spontaneously initiated Swamiji into his lineage, during which she fell into a deep trance-like state. Sweets and nuts then began dropping from the ceiling and appearing from nowhere, as though they were on springs, and started bouncing around us. In all, there were seven of us present that day to witness this phenomenon: myself, my friend, another working medium, a receptionist from the Arthur Findlay College, Jammu's interpreter, Swamiji, and Jammu himself.

While all the above things were happening, the door to the room kept opening and closing by itself and children's footsteps and laughter could be heard outside in the corridor, even though there was no one else in the building. The atmosphere was joyous and alive and we found ourselves lost in laughter at what was happening. Jammu asked, via the interpreter, why we were laughing. We replied that it was because of what we were witnessing was making us feel happy and joyful and giving us a sense of elevation. "Don't you realise, it is you who are doing this, not I. It's your energy that's creating it", he replied via the interpreter.

The five of us who went that day were looked upon auspiciously by Swamiji because of there being five Pandava brothers that are mentioned in one of India's most holy books, *The Bhagavad Gita*.

On another occasion, I remember talking to a young, wealthy and well-educated Indian couple in the waiting area in the living room and they told me their story about how they had come to see Jammu and had become great devotees of his. They told me that numerous doctors had told them they would be unable to have any children and that the problem of conception was to do with the husband. When Jammu met them, he told them exactly why they had come before uttering a single word to him. He then pointed to the floor and at their feet there was a herb that had suddenly materialised. Maharaj told them to steep it into a glass of water and drink it, then put more water in and keep drinking it for seven days. Soon after, Maharaj told the couple at their first meeting with him, the lady would become pregnant and give birth to twin boys, which would be their only children, and how this was a blessing from God. The young couple told me how everything happened exactly as Jammu had predicted.

There was one occasion when a friend of my friend, who was in his late 60s and a Religious Studies PhD student and member of the Buddhist community at Plum Village in France, went to see Maharaj. Like many academics, he was slightly sceptical. While in the presence of Jammu Maharaj, Jammu asked him to meditate and as he did, he distinctly heard the sound of *om* vibrating around him and had what could only be described as a change in his awareness. Unfortunately, he then had to dash off afterwards without eating anything (food was usually given freely to visitors) and went to continue some research he was doing at the School of Oriental and African Studies in London. When he arrived at the university, he told others what he had just experienced, but then began to feel dizzy. Luckily, one of his colleagues knew something about such things and about the transference of energies that take place with great yogis, and how it was *important to eat afterwards*, which he then did and instantly started to feel less light-headed and more grounded.

A friend of mine, a wealthy business man who was interested in Yogic teachings, also used to visit Jammu regularly. On his first visit, he turned up unannounced. Yet he was told by Jammu why he had gone to see him. Jammu then continued to tell him all about his life and his spiritual unfoldment. Everything that was said was totally accurate. This first meeting with Jammu had such a profound effect on him that even later in the day, various business acquaintances who had no interest in such things as Yoga masters remarked how different he looked – how he looked almost radiant, and asked him what had brought about the sudden change in his appearance!

One known medium who went to see Jammu about her spiritual and mediumistic development was disappointed because when she tried to ask about her unfoldment, Jammu began to gently tap her on her sides with his stick and replied, "I'm not interested in this at this time as I am more concerned about the blood", and began to work on trying to heal the condition. Incredibly, what Jammu had not been told before, was that the medium suffered from severe diabetes.

On one occasion, when I went to see Jammu, his son told me that his father was upstairs resting. I did not want to disturb him, so I told his son that I would leave, but as I got up, I heard Jammu calling me and insisting that I go up to the bedroom where he was resting. As I entered the room, he was lying on an Indian style truckle bed with a pillow placed upon it. Apart from the bed, which I could see under, the room was completely bare. After spending some time with Jammu and discussing various things, he then materialised an apple in his hand and gave it to me. He then held out his hand again and said he needed another one, which instantly appeared. All this happened in broad daylight. I asked him how he could do this and I could not.

At that point his son entered the room with a smile on his face after interpreting a few words his father had just spoken and said, "My father is telling me that it happens because he knows he is one with God". Jammu then smiled, chuckled and looked at me with his piercing eyes and said, "You just believe you are Glyn".

Jammu's grandchildren who lived at the centre told me how they always looked forward to their grandfather coming as their home would smell and feel different. Even the food tasted better when he was there, they told me. It was only after his passing that I began to learn just how esteemed he really was. He was apparently a wealthy man who had financed the building of many temples throughout India and an ashram in Jammu in Northern India where he came from, near Kashmir. He helped to open my spiritual eyes and mind to wider and more inclusive visions of what was possible within me. My meetings with him transformed my spiritual life, which, for me, has always naturally flowed into my mediumistic work and cannot be separated.

\* \* \*

## Quotations by Glyn Edwards

*We must embrace the light that shines through other faiths, other ways of thinking and traditions.*
*An open mind to others is essential.*
*~ Realms of Wondrous Gifts*

\* \* \*

*In the beginning it may not be clear that changes are starting to happen. But with patience and openness we begin to see where our previous patterns of thought end and another realm of understanding and activity is starting to unfold and guide us.*
*~ Spirit Gems*

\* \* \*

*Spiritual teachings often highlight how we are essentially a spirit with a body – that we are in fact 'already' living in a spirit world – and how our perceptions simply need to open in order to discover this truth for ourselves.*
*~ The Potential of Mediumship (expanded edition)*

\* \* \*

*Each of us is a unique part of life. For the brief time we are here on Earth we may see further than material egocentric life and recognise that we and all life are manifestations of an essential spiritual source.*
*~ The Potential of Mediumship (expanded edition)*

\* \* \*

# Quotations by Glyn Edwards

*By deepening our understanding we realise that all is interconnected and are parts of one great ocean of life.*
*~ Spirit Gems*

\* \* \*

*If we accept that life is eternal and there are other realms of existence intertwined with our physical world, then it must be a natural step in our evolution to be able to communicate with these other realms and with those who are living on.*
*~ The Potential of Mediumship*

\* \* \*

*In the past we may have been influenced in our thinking by the beliefs of others. Now we must take the opportunity to discover for ourselves their truth or falsehood.*
*~ The Spirit World in Plain English*

\* \* \*

*As we enter into development with an open mind and a willingness to grow into spiritual maturity, which means including the inevitable difficulties and suffering we and others encounter, along with blissful moments of awakening to divinity, we begin to realise that all life is ultimately One – that there is no clear division between set systems of belief or everyday life and spiritual understanding.*
*~ Realms of Wondrous Gifts*

\* \* \*

# 5
# Realms of Knowing

*This chapter is a creatively edited compilation of several sections from two series of popular recordings Glyn did in the first half of the 1990s.[1] It includes a workshop section designed by Glyn in 2013.*

In the development of mediumship, it is essential to have the right conditions for communication with the spirit to happen. Our role as mediums in this process is important because it is *we* who in fact build the power needed from our side of life for spirit communication to take place. In this, we must understand that we ourselves are also spirit. We also need to understand the importance of the aura, and how we can build spiritual and psychic energy so a stronger link between us and the spirit world can occur.

Difficulties that are sometimes encountered in the unfoldment of mediumship are often created by a lack of the right kind of preparation. The spirit world requires us to get ourselves, our mind, feelings, aspirations and life in tune with one another and settled before working mediumistically. Having said this, I have

---

1. Transcribing spoken words into written sentences is more of an art of capturing key points of what someone said and their distinctive choice of terms and phrases (though in some places a clearer word has been added) and putting them into coherent grammatical form without unnecessary repetition, instead of simply typing out word-for-word the way things were said. Some sections have been moved to fit others, and linking phrases have been added in places to introduce or join passages or refer back to a previous point made for the purpose of helping the reading flow and gel as a unified written chapter.

no doubt that if we are open to the spirit's influence, the spirit will always assist us in attuning to their world. For ultimately, we are not just our physical body but also an eternal spirit that is a part of the spirit world, and all we need to do is awaken to this reality. An essential part of this process is in realising that all life and things house within them the light that many call the Divine Spirit/God, and that we live, move and have our being in this reality. And because this reality permeates all things, seen and unseen, we are never outside of its/God's presence. By fostering stillness and focused awareness, we awaken to this omnipresent truth. We will also find that these key skills serve us well in mediumistic development.

For in mediumistic unfoldment, we need stillness and a concentrative mind that can maintain awareness of the spirit world and can let go of other levels of thought that interfere with spirit communication. Although it ought to be mentioned here that it is in fact a joint effort between us and the spirit, which links us and the spirit with the law of cause and effect as well as the law of association. The more skilled we are in being aware of different levels of being and the changes that take place during mediumistic work, the more open we will be to the spirit's influence and numerous experiences and realms of unfoldment. And when we include the whole of ourself in this process, not just one or two facets of unfoldment, we awaken to both the spirit world and the Divine and their influence more deeply.

### The Oneness of Spirit

The ultimate cause and creator of our being is the Divine Spirit, which connects us with the all-ness of Nature and Mother Earth. The spirit world, which is interwoven with the Divine, permeates everything. Every living thing and species that exists is a part of the spirit world. The natural world is an expression of the Divine's creation. And what Nature is, we also are; for we are also unique parts of Nature and expressions of divinity. So in the process of our development, we have to recognise our relationship with the physical world as well as non-physical dimensions of spirituality.

Linked to this understanding is the role of the breath, which connects with Nature, her various elements, and with our ability to be still and quiet in mind and body. This is not about making our mind blank but working with and building energy through our breath and working with our auric field in order to become sensitive to changes in vibrations that happen when we awaken to the power of our breath and the aura's activity. By doing this, we begin to work with the flow of our breath, which is in fact a form of energy. Through this, we then start to become more sensitive to and aware of changes in vibrations that occur – including energies that can even weaken us – and positive changes in energy that the spirit world create as they blend with us and make themselves known through our auric field and our mediumistic senses.

The deeper we are able to go with the natural flow of our unfoldment and awaken to the presence of the spirit, we discover more ways of opening to an array of spiritual, psychic and mediumistic powers that we possess. For authentic mediumship never remains on one level. It involves moving from various levels to others, from the realms of the physical senses to other realms of being, consciousness and knowing. A key thing to remember is that there is no limit to the spirit that we are. We therefore need to be aware of any imposed limitations we or others may have placed upon our unfoldment. It is important to realise this as we are not dealing with physical senses, which have their limitations, but ultimately with our spirit senses, which are limitless.

In mediumship, we do not receive information through our physical eyes or ears but through mediumistic spheres of knowledge, which stimulate conscious levels of our being and help us to recognise changes happening during spirit communication. It is about searching within and reaching out to other dimensions of life that interconnect with our physical realm of existence.

## Practical Unfoldment

Ultimately, mediumistic unfoldment encompasses practical living. Within the experiences and abilities that surface in the process of mediumship, it is important to embrace things that are essential to everyday living. At its deepest level, the act of mediumship seeks to enhance our daily life and helps us to be of selfless service to others. Therefore, a harmonious integration between everyday life and our mediumship is important to include in unfoldment. Through this, we begin the ongoing journey of refining who we are, and refining our awareness and attunement to the spirit world and its enriching influence. From my own experiences as a medium, I have often noticed how mediumship is enhanced by the ability to be open to spiritual attributes such as creativity, compassion and discernment. I believe the more we can naturally open to and manifest these, the closer we will be to blending naturally with the spirit world.

The underlying teachings of the spirit are about awakening to the Oneness of all life and becoming co-creators with the spirit and the Divine expressing their creativity. No matter what our beliefs or religion, we are never separate from this activity. And by embracing the wondrous creative unity of life, comes a heightened awareness of the presence of the spirit and the Divine revealing themselves in and through all things. For the spirit world and the

Divine are obviously not bound to just mediumistic realms of ability. This is not about being pious but about practical spiritual living and understanding. These various realms of awakening, being and knowing have for many years been important to me as a medium, have continuously helped me with my mediumistic abilities, and guided me in numerous areas of my life.

## Awareness of a Greater Whole

In Spiritualism we tend to look at unfoldment as being about awareness of the spirit world but teach little about awareness of our own authentic spirit. I believe we should never undervalue reflecting upon the spirit that we are, as it is important for our spiritual understanding and growth. Communicators in the spirit world often remind us that we are a deathless, sacred living spirit and often seek to encourage us to contemplate the implications of this knowledge and turn it into wholesome actions such as caring for all life and people, including ourselves.

We know for instance that the spirit is the life force, and without it the body dies. Much of what we are aware of in Spiritualism is often limited to what we traditionally call mediumship. However, I feel our awareness needs to encompass a greater whole of who and what we are. By this, I do not simply mean the body, the emotions and the intellect, but also other realms connected with intuition and an array of essential areas of spirituality and spiritual living. Although intuition connects strongly with mediumistic gifts, it also connects with different abilities of seeing and knowing. Intuition is in fact a natural part of everyone's being that functions in numerous ways – as feelings, states of knowing and creativity, and in spiritual awakenings. How often have you met someone for the first time and have had an instant feeling about him or her that tells you not to trust that person? Our responses to Nature and her beauty also link us with intuition. Strongly gifted people are often highly intuitive. It is said that Mozart heard complete symphonies in his head and then simply wrote them down, which happened through the use of his intuitive abilities.

We must look at life from all levels. And ==within mediumistic unfoldment, look for not only what can be described as provable facts but for what can also be included and encouraged for the purpose of holistic and wholesome growth.== If we do not do this, we are limiting our understanding of everything that the spirit is about. This is why we need to develop an awareness that is constantly evolving. Included in this is the ability to be deeply aware of the physical world in which we live and its awesome creativity. Unfortunately, we often do not make time to stop and reflect upon how various creative realms of life can positively influence us, and how we are interrelated with the natural world and its workings. Embracing wider levels of awareness and different realms of our mind, body, feelings and creativity is essential for healthy unfoldment. For this reason, I believe it is important to include contemporary findings of science and psychology in our development, as they can help us to understand parts of our being and how we can respond to life in more caring, wholesome, harmonious and appreciative ways.

When we become more open to life, we heighten our abilities to become more sensitively aware of all things within and around us. This, if we are open to allowing it to happen, can then lead us into realms of change and transformation – to embracing who we truly are and ways in which we can wholesomely grow. Such awakenings deeply lead us to life as an ongoing meditation, to the eternity of our existence, and the empowering Divine Spirit in all.

\* \* \*

## Things to Consider for Mediumistic Unfoldment
### Workshop Steps

Mediumistic unfoldment is by its very nature an individual experience. We cannot so much teach someone to be a medium but support, assist and offer guidance about awareness of potential abilities, and give advice about being openly receptive to ongoing unfoldment. It is important to remember that gifts of observation, discernment and stillness need to be cultivated in order to awaken to the spirit. The following are some beneficial steps to consider:

1. Be aware of the rhythm of your breath and let it find its own natural rhythm (do not control the breath).
2. Set the intention of seeking to unfold your mediumship.
3. Seek the guidance of the spirit and be receptive to what they are seeking to achieve – observe how their influence can naturally flow into and enrich your whole life.
4. Find time to be still and reflect upon the spirit.
5. Embrace all things that happen in your unfoldment with wise discernment and objectivity.
6. Realise that the spirit world honours your natural intelligence and discernment. In return, foster respect for the spirit world's wisdom.
7. Cultivate an openness of mind and a compassionate heart.
8. Allow yourself, through experiences you undergo, to develop trust, receptiveness and willingness in mediumistic unfoldment.
9. Honour your mediumistic growth as something sacred that can help and encourage you, other people, life, and the spirit world to manifest and express their love and wisdom more fully in the world.

# Quotations by Glyn Edwards

*Spirituality is not an escape from one world into another but an inclusion of the whole of life.*
*~ The Potential of Mediumship (expanded edition)*

\* \* \*

*Early indigenous people and shamans were the first humans to connect with a spirit world permeating Nature and to communicate with their departed ancestors.*
*Others have looked towards the more transcendent areas of spirituality. Although there are some who have never completely separated themselves from some of the early indigenous beliefs and practices, there are some who have, which has led to an unhealthy separation between Nature and spirit.*
*~ Realms of Wondrous Gifts*

\* \* \*

*Ultimately there is no true separation between people and other life, either in this life or after physical death. We are essentially one spirit that is without boundaries and interconnected equally with all.*
*~ The Potential of Mediumship (expanded edition)*

\* \* \*

*[Through] an authentic understanding of what mediumship can truly mean in the here and now of contemporary life … we may then, with open minds, allow ourselves to present the intention to serve the spirit world in the truest ways we can.*
*~ The Potential of Mediumship (expanded edition)*

\* \* \*

# 6
# Exercises

*The following introduction and last exercise are from an unreleased recording Glyn made in 2010.[1] The first two exercises are from a popular series of recordings he released in 1994. It also includes two workshop sections designed by Glyn in 2013.*

Those searching to understand mediumistic awareness and how to communicate better with the spirit world, need to realise that ultimately the answers to unfoldment are to be found within themselves – within an emerging and awakening awareness of those in the spirit world working and interacting with them. Yet I should mention that unfoldment also includes our daily interactions with life, with others and with the natural world of which we are amazing parts. It is by being open to all things that we in fact awaken to wider, more wholesome and inclusive changes in our growth, which then help us to move healthily forward in our development.

When you sit for mediumistic unfoldment, it is a time for you to experience, observe and reflect upon how you are affected by different states of consciousness, how you can awaken to your own spirit, the powers of all life and the evolving and creative Universe that Earth itself is a part, and what all these things mean to you. It is a time and opportunity for being aware of how

---

1. The recording was never made available as Glyn was tired when he did it and this was noticeable on the recording. The introduction and all the exercises have been especially edited for this chapter.

you relate to the infinite powers of the spirit and your own eternal Self, through which you can investigate your interconnections with the spirit – seeing how the spirit works within and through you, guides and inspires you, and how, through you, the spirit can deeply touch, guide and inspire others. This includes an ongoing receptivity and openness to your interrelationship with the Divine, with the continuous creativity of life and the omnipresence of the spirit world, which leads to a profound realisation of wholeness and unity, and acknowledging not only your mediumistic potential but your spiritual interrelationships with all. Within this journey, you will come to honour and trust those that work with you in the spirit world. You will also come to recognise the sacred oneness of life.

As new awareness reveals itself, you will realise new truths. The life you may have lived so far might even come into conflict with fresher and wider fields of vision that require time to integrate before finding harmonious balance. Ultimately, it is a quest about spiritual discovery, insights and freedom, through which you will experience numerous beneficial transformations.

In my own understanding, mediumship is not about seeking to be a particular type of medium. It is a journey and awakening through numerous spheres of activity and experience that assist us in being more openly receptive to infinite positive potential, and allowing that potential to surface and shine more purely and unrestrictively through all that we do and are. I trust you will discover this for yourself and many other joyful and life affirming experiences on your quest. Realise that as you begin the following exercises, you are taking great steps forward in bringing about a variety of wondrous mediumistic and spiritual changes within you. I wish you many blessings on your journey.

\* \* \*

As the following exercises have various sections to them, you may like to ask a friend to lead you through them or record yourself reading them and then meditate to your recording. Be sure to leave an appropriate length of space between the different sections if you do this.

**Exercise 1: Developing Sensitivity and Awareness**

**1.** Sit in an upright position with your feet, if seated on a chair, firmly on the ground, and the palms of your hands upwards, one over the other in a relaxed position on your lap. Close your eyes and think of the word "relaxation" and feel yourself relaxing for a few minutes.

**2.** As you relax, become aware of your breathing. Observe the in- and out-breath. Be aware and sense the difference of breathing in a positive sense of peacefulness and calmness and breathing out any negativity you may be holding within you. Take a few minutes to do this and become aware of your feelings as you do it.

**3.** Once you are relaxed and filled with a sense of peacefulness, calmness and positive frame of mindfulness, become aware of what feelings come from this sublime state of conscious awareness. Stay with your feelings for a few minutes.

**4.** Now become aware of the reality of living, moving and being in God – aware that divinity is right where you are and its power is an intrinsic part of you. As you do this, be aware of what this is awakening within your consciousness – of anything that you feel or sense. Stay with your feelings and senses for a few minutes.

5. As you recognise your God Self, the Divine presence within, remind yourself that you are relaxed, and filled with peacefulness, calmness and positive energy.

6. Bring your attention to the middle of your chest and visualise a light emanating from your heart. As you see this light, become aware that it is gradually expanding and moving downwards to the abdomen, the solar plexus, and upwards to the upper chest and throat. And then slowly expanding more to the legs, feet, shoulders, arms and head. At this point you will come to recognise that the light is the light of your own spirit – that your spirit is a body of light. Sense and feel the truth of this within yourself. Stay with your senses and feelings for a few minutes.

7. Become aware of the light of your own spirit expanding further outwards from you and filling the space around you. As this happens, you will become less aware of your physical self and more aware of non-physical realms and sensitivity. Whatever you become aware of at this stage, let it occur naturally. Observe what is happening and what you are awakening to. Your aim at this point is to seek the influence of the spirit world. You will notice that the light that is expanding is assisting you in this goal. Notice any changes in your awareness, and in your senses and feelings of different vibrations and energies. Stay with any changes you notice for approximately 10 minutes.

8. Come back gently to your physical surroundings and consciousness. Try to retain all that you have experienced during this exercise, with a feeling of being refreshed, relaxed and at peace with yourself. In order to solidify your experiences, share them with others you may have been sitting with or make a

mental or physical note of all that happened in the exercise if you were sitting alone. This period of silence has been for you to attune to the spirit. Realise that you have taken a huge step forward in your unfoldment.

* * *

### Exercise 2: Mediumistic and Spiritual Attunement

**1.** Sit in an upright position with your feet, if seated on a chair, firmly on the ground, and the palms of your hands upwards, one over the other in a relaxed position on your lap. Close your eyes and become aware of the rhythm of your breathing – of breathing in and out. Enjoy this activity for a few minutes.

**2.** Keep your attention on the in- and out-breath. Mentally and slowly go through all parts of your body from the feet to the top of your head. Take time to mentally/silently tell each part of your physical body that it is relaxed and release any tensions with the out-breath. When you have finished doing this, mentally tell yourself that you are at peace and completely relaxed and become one with the peace and relaxed state you have created.

**3.** In your mind, formulate some thoughts about the spirit, why you are sitting, what you require of the spirit and need help with. Let your thoughts blend with the spirit and ask the spirit world to help you be aware of their presence. Do not force this, but do it with a sense of depth, receptivity and sincerity. Stay with any feelings or impressions for a few minutes.

**4.** Now talk to the Great Spirit – use whatever term for God/divinity you feel most comfortable with – in order to seek its/his/her/the Divine's blessing and help in your unfoldment. Take a few minutes to do this and to be still and, once again, become aware of your breath's *natural rhythm* gently flowing in and out. Do not force your breathing. Just let it flow naturally.

5. You have now made a mental act of attunement. Sit now with a sense of relaxed expectancy and openness. Become more involved in anything that may unfold during this time. If anything occurs, let it naturally happen. Ask those that work with you in the spirit world what any occurrence means but do not worry about an answer if one does not come – just let yourself become one with the stillness and silence of this exercise and with your attunement. Whatever changes occur, let them happen without forcing them. You may feel a presence or see colours. If you do, then welcome those experiences and continue to be receptive to any other experiences – acknowledging them while remaining open to further impressions and experience. Embrace your oneness with the spirit world. Stay in this relaxed and silent state of attunement for approximately 10 to 15 minutes.

6. Come back gently to your physical surroundings and consciousness. Try to retain all that you have experienced during this exercise, with a feeling of being refreshed, relaxed and at peace with yourself. In order to solidify your experiences, share them with others you may have been sitting with or make a mental or physical note of all that happened in the exercise if you were sitting alone.

\* \* \*

## Exercise 3: Awakening to the Power and Energy of the Spirit

**1.** Give yourself time to be still and allow any tensions of the day to drift away from you. Close your eyes and become aware of your breath as it gently flows in and out. Become filled with the sense of how wonderful it is to breathe – that breathing in and out connects with a force and power of life: that every part of you, such as your awareness, feelings, actions and reactions, connect with the breath.

**2.** Allow your breath to become rhythmic and stable, surrender to its flow and know that you can begin a new beginning. As you breathe out, let go of the past. Every time that you breathe in, silently affirm to yourself, "I am breathing in a new beginning", and as you breathe out, silently affirm, "I am breathing out and letting go of the past". As you do this, truly realise that you can bring about a new beginning and let go of any negativity or restrictions in your life.

**3.** Feel, on the in-breath, the power and energy of the in-breath, and the power of a new beginning blending with the whole of your being.

**4.** As you breathe out, feel the energy of your past and the healing energy that comes in letting it go. In surrendering to this, you will start to live in the present moment and will become liberated in your mind and feelings. Stay with this for a few minutes.

**5.** Realise that your in- and out-breath is power, and that this power is within you. And how your mind and body are directing your in- and out-breath and aiding a new beginning and assisting in letting go of past associations.

**6.** As you focus on your in- and out-breath, notice how your mind comes into harmony with your breathing and brings about a state of tranquil quietness and stillness. Become one with this state, and aware of it in your mind and feelings. Realise that this feeling of quietness and stillness is power – a power, vibration and energy that is within you and around you. Blend with this experience and be alive to everything that happens for a few minutes.

**7.** As the quietness and stillness becomes more established, you will realise that the whole of your awareness is awakening you to your spirit Self and opening you to all that is within you and around you. You may experience it as an expansion, a quickening in vibration or as a thought, feeling or deep knowing. Whatever begins to occur, allow it to unfold in its own unique way. Do not restrict yourself to ideas of there being a set way for awakening to the spirit Self to occur. Trust your experience and allow it to flow in its own direction.

You may feel yourself expanding, filling the room you are in and filling your heart. You may feel yourself floating above or below yourself, see colours, hear a sound or feel a change in temperature. Just be aware of these things and aware that the experiences are a part of you. Feel the flow of energy, vibration and power of each moment. Go with whatever occurs. And as you perceive things happening, realise you have become aware of a timeless and spaceless realm.

Stay with your experiences and be conscious of everything that happens for a few minutes.

8. Become aware that this timeless and spaceless realm is intertwined with the Earth (of which you are a wondrous part), and the Earth's energy, vibration and power. Notice this energy, vibration and power building within and around you, and how it adds to your spiritual empowerment. Realise you are interconnected with everything in Nature – that all the powers of creation in the natural world are within you. You are the Divine in life and are limitless. This is your true Self. And within you and Nature is the Universe in miniature. As you open to this cosmic power within you, your mind will begin to open and associate with the limitlessness of your being and your energies, vibrations and powers. As you do so, the spirit world that walks and interconnects with you will become more joyous in your progress because they will be able to work with and through you in more openly natural ways. Stay with any experiences you have of these things for a few minutes.

9. You have now awakened to a Source that is eternal and brings into life harmony, wholeness and healing. At this stage, your own spirit will take you to a world beyond regular states of knowing and feeling, to a realm of being where spirit people work with and through you. Welcome them and know that you are also welcomed by them. Know that you are one with them.

Here you awaken to the personalities, thoughts and guidance of those that work with you. Notice that as you awaken more to this level that interlinks with you, that the energies, vibrations and powers of your own being, your own spirit Self, become stronger. Stay with your experiences for a few minutes.

10. As you associate with the world of the spirit more deeply and profoundly, be aware of any impressions or senses of seeing,

hearing or feeling of those that work with you in the spirit. Lay aside any doubts you may have and trust your awareness. Stay in this attuned state for approximately 10 to 15 minutes.

**11.** Come back gently to your physical surroundings and consciousness. Realise that this exercise has brought about a new beginning, a realisation of the oneness you share with the spirit and the creative Divine Principle interwoven with all.

\* \* \*

***Affirmation***
*Goodness and creativity flow in me, through me and from me. I am a part of the creative force that works in and through all life. As this power is an intrinsic part of who I am, I claim a life of continuous and eternal growth. I accept and acknowledge my good and my creative spiritual potential and continually work towards expressing them fully in my life.*
~ From *Spirit Gems*

\* \* \*

## Your Interrelationship with Earth Life and the Spirit World

### Workshop Reflection

Take time to reflect upon the below bullet points, then consider the five questions/reflections:

- Awareness, self-knowledge, collective and individual responsibility and wisdom.
- Moderation in things that are not essential to spiritual living.
- Authenticity in thoughts, speech and actions.
- Unconditional reverence for all life.
- Understanding there is no *thing* or *one* (human or more-than-human) that can be seen as "other" – as being separate from you – and that all life and things are created from an original source of goodness.

### Questions/Reflections

1. How can you awaken to and live any of the above?
2. Are any of them already important to you?
3. What do you understand about the implications of mediumistic unfoldment and there being a spirit world and divinity interwoven with all?
4. What is ethical, altruistic and spiritual to you?
5. Are there any areas in particular that you feel passionate about or feel you need to embrace and work on?
6. What can you do to be more spiritually engaged with Earth life?

*Write down your thoughts, impressions, feelings and responses, and ways that you can manifest them as creative forces in your everyday life and unfoldment.*

## A Kaleidoscope of Mediumship
### Workshop Reflection

Within mediumship we often talk of clairsentience (clear sensing), clairvoyance (clear seeing) and clairaudience (clear hearing). Yet we often forget to mention other areas such as claircognisance (clear knowing), clairalience (clear smelling) and clairgustance (clear tasting). In addition to these, there are of course some forms of healing, along with physical and trance mediumship to consider. There are also other realms that are often not traditionally recognised under the banner of mediumship. Some of which could be listed as below. After reading each one of them, ask yourself how you might interpret it as a form of mediumship, how it interconnects with the others, how you can awaken to it, and what it might imply and bring about within your unfoldment:

- The mediumship of individual exploration
- The mediumship of meditative and contemplative awareness
- The mediumship of energy and vibration
- The mediumship of light and colour
- The mediumship of mindful wisdom
- The mediumship of life and engaged spiritual living
- The mediumship of compassionate actions
- The mediumship of creativity
- The mediumship of Nature
- The mediumship of mysticism
- The mediumship of universal cosmic consciousness

## Quotations by Glyn Edwards

*The more we know ourselves, the more we transform ourselves and the more the spirit world flows naturally through and within us.*
*~ Spirit Gems*

\* \* \*

*When you sit quietly and become aware of the spirit within and as this awareness becomes stronger, realise that this inner spirit Self has its being in God – that God is within you and in all things, and how all things are ultimately in God.*
*~ The Spirit World in Plain English*

\* \* \*

*It is God and the spirit working through our individuality, character and personality that needs be the ground on which our unfoldment begins.*
*~ The Spirit World in Plain English*

\* \* \*

*Don't let fear enter your unfoldment, as there is ultimately nothing to be afraid of. The world of the spirit will join with you, and through this blending, you will find many wonderful and beautiful experiences that will enrich your life and the great work that lies ahead.*
*~ The Potential of Mediumship*

\* \* \*

## Quotations by Glyn Edwards

*Living by spiritual laws means going beyond ordinary laws, taking responsibility for every area of our lives – our thoughts, feelings and actions – and being respectful of everyone and every form of life with which we come into contact.
We may not be able to accomplish this overnight, but it is in the trying that we become more caring, loving, centred, responsible and empowered spiritual beings.*
~ Spirit Gems

\* \* \*

*What can often seem like wrong turns, false starts or mistakes might discourage us. But invariably these things help us to refine our awareness and lead us to firmer convictions about the paths we must tread.*
~ The Potential of Mediumship

\* \* \*

*We must realise that our true spirit Self is whole and without boundaries, and continually seeks to express this wholeness and boundless nature in and through every level of our being and everything that we do.
It knows no limitations and has the power to bring about positive changes, congruence in the ways we think, feel and act and enhance all creative abilities and qualities of compassion we have.*
~ Spirit Gems

\* \* \*

# Afterword

**Writing with Glyn**
*by Santoshan (Stephen Wollaston)*

Shortly after I first met Glyn, a graphics partnership I had in London Docklands moved into computerised design work. I mentioned to Glyn that if he wanted to write and publish something, this was the time, as the technology made book-layout less expensive. As an energetic and creative young man as Glyn was, he instantly proposed that we write a book *together*, which I wasn't expecting, on different areas of spirituality and mediumship.

Glyn's input was amazing. He seemed to have no end of experience, wisdom and new perspective to add. Then synchronicity magically played a part when it was finished, as a call came through from the then editor of Psychic News, Tony Ortzen, scouting for a publisher, who asked Glyn if he would like to write a book. He quickly replied, "Steve and I have just finished one". We later revised and updated it in 2011 and gave it a more contemporary title than it previously had. Glyn was extremely pleased with the look and reading of the revised edition, which is clearly seen in his opening Acknowledgments.

After completing the first title, I had an idea for a workbook

---

Note: This Afterword is from the anthology of Glyn's wisdom *The Potential of Mediumship (expanded edition)*, with extra information from a requested article for Psychic News, published in July 2015.

and this time approached Glyn about writing it together. We also revised and expanded it in 2011 and gave it a different title to what the previous publisher had given it. Once again, Glyn displayed how pithy he could be in putting great insights together. In the final section of the book, we found various quotations to put in on important spheres of unfoldment, which Glyn had no end of enthusiasm in finding key teachings from different writers and teachers he loved.

He then asked if I would put together a book on mediumistic and psychic powers in different traditions, as he wanted to promote a more inclusive and open-minded understanding of alternative paths amongst his students.

Having already written an article for an appendix that touched on this in a Yoga book with a swami, I accepted his request and expanded what I'd started in the other book but asked Glyn if he would also like to be interviewed for two large sections that could be included. He said he would. Questions put to him were invariably followed by a period of reflective silence. He would then answer fluently without pausing until he had covered all that he felt was needed to be said.

The anthology *The Potential of Mediumship* I suggested to Glyn about putting together. Glyn did a book launch for it after a truly dazzling public demonstration of his mediumship on 18th September 2012 at the Eastbourne Centre, East Sussex, and sold almost every copy we had with us. The queue to the table where Glyn sat joyously chatting and signing copies for everyone was a sight to be seen. Putting the book together for him was a labour of love, and I was really happy to see it turned out to be such a big success for him that day. I will certainly miss doing the creative projects we did together and those wonderful memorable times we had.

\* \* \*

# Books & Recordings *by or with* Glyn Edwards

128 page expanded edition
ISBN 978-0-9569210-3-1

*eBook edition available from Amazon and Smashwords. Hardback edition also available.*

## THE POTENTIAL OF MEDIUMSHIP
### A Collection of Essential Teachings and Exercises (expanded edition)
Glyn Edwards
Compiled and with an introduction by Santoshan (Stephen Wollaston)

Presents an inspiring collection of teachings, along with numerous essential exercises for unfolding mediumistic and spiritual gifts. In this first ever anthology of Glyn's wisdom, he shared first-hand accounts about his own mediumistic experiences and imparted profound insights that will help you to move forward with your abilities. There are chapters here for beginners and the more advanced that reveal how the spirit world can communicate with and work through us and prove survival of life after death.

'There should be many more books like this!'
~ Psychic News

'A book well worth studying, especially for the added spiritual dimension.'
~ Two Worlds magazine

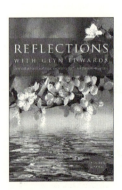

Mid-price paperback
140 page expanded edition
ISBN 978-1080308798

*Mid-price eBook edition available from Amazon and Smashwords. Hardback edition also available.*

## REFLECTIONS WITH GLYN EDWARDS
Compiled and with Additional Material by Santoshan (Stephen Wollaston)

A meditations book of profound and inspiring quotations by Glyn Edwards, who was internationally acclaimed as one of the finest motivational speakers and demonstrators of mediumship in the UK. This beautiful book uses an array of passages from his published works and was released to coincide with what would have been Glyn's 70th Earth-year.

'His insight into and experience of an array of interrelated realms of spirituality was unquestionably phenomenal and deeply profound.'
~ From the compiler's introduction

160 pages
ISBN 78-0-9569210-0-0

*eBook edition available from Amazon and Smashwords. Hardback edition also available.*

## THE SPIRIT WORLD IN PLAIN ENGLISH
**Mediumistic and Spiritual Unfoldment**
Glyn Edwards and Santoshan (Stephen Wollaston)
Foreword by Don Hills

*The Spirit World in Plain English* is a revised and updated edition of the authors' first book. In this beneficial manual, Glyn Edwards and Santoshan share practical exercises and teachings for discovering inherent mediumistic and spiritual potential. Together, they combine their knowledge in far-reaching ways and cover numerous essentials for understanding and interacting with the ever-present world of the spirit.

**'This book is more than just another book on spiritual and psychic development; it's literally the bible on development.'**
~ Amazon UK (customer review of first edition)

128 pages
ISBN 978-0-9569210-1-7

*eBook edition available from Amazon and Smashwords. Hardback edition also available.*

## SPIRIT GEMS
**Essential Guidance for Spiritual, Mediumistic and Creative Unfoldment**
Glyn Edwards and Santoshan (Stephen Wollaston)

*Spirit Gems* is a revised and expanded edition of the authors' second book, which provides practical steps for discovering how to live more freely, deeply and peacefully. Glyn Edwards and Santoshan write beautifully whilst covering essentials such as living in the now, facing our fears, finding unity with all and harmonising the whole of ourselves. Both authors share profound insights for immersing our lives in spiritually and mediumistically centred living. Their down-to-earth wisdom weaves skilfully through various levels of individual unfoldment and enriching realms of transforming experience.

**'A must for anyone's bookshelf.'**
~ The Greater World Newsletter (review of first edition)

## REALMS OF WONDROUS GIFTS
Psychic, Mediumistic and Miraculous Powers in the Great Mystical and Wisdom Traditions (revised and redesigned edition)
Santoshan (Stephen Wollaston)
With conversations with Glyn Edwards

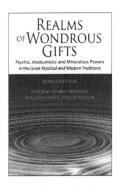

Low-cost paperback
157 pages
ISBN 978-1658935630

Low-cost eBook edition available from Amazon and Smashwords.
Hardback edition also available.

*Realms of Wondrous Gifts* presents an in-depth look at psychic, mediumistic and miraculous powers in the world's great mystical and wisdom traditions, and includes key insights into various teachings and practices. It also includes two extensive conversations with Glyn Edwards, in which he eloquently shared far-reaching thoughts on several interwoven facets of development.

'A real gem of a book ... Highly recommended.'
~ Psychic World

'A rare and enriching book.'
~ Eileen Davies, internationally renowned medium and spiritual teacher

---

## AUDIO CDs BY AND DOWNLOADS OF GLYN EDWARDS

Audio CDs by Glyn Edwards available from
the Mind-Body-Spirit Online website:
www.mindbodyspiritonline.co.uk
Tel: (01202) 267684 (outside UK: +441202 267684)

Downloads of CDs by Glyn Edwards available from:
www.listening2spirit.com

---

Glyn Edwards remembered website:
https://glynedwards.wixsite.com/glynedwards

Made in the USA
Middletown, DE
14 October 2022